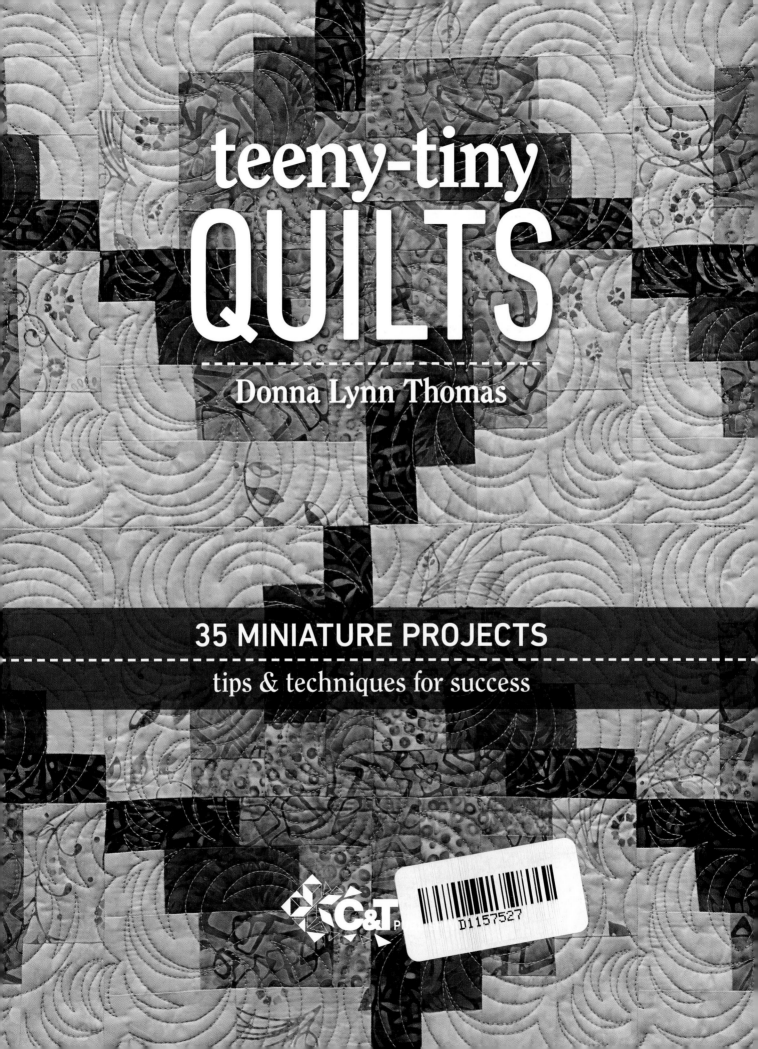

teeny-tiny
QUILTS

Donna Lynn Thomas

35 MINIATURE PROJECTS

tips & techniques for success

Text copyright © 2018 by Donna Lynn Thomas

Photography and artwork copyright © 2018 by C&T Publishing, Inc.

Publisher: Amy Marson

Creative Director: Gailen Runge

Editors: Christine Doyle and Lynn Koolish

Technical Editor: Debbie Rodgers

Cover/Book Designer: April Mostek

Production Coordinator: Tim Manibusan

Production Editor: Alice Mace Nakanishi

Illustrator: Linda Johnson

Cover photography by Lucy Glover

Style photography by Lucy Glover and instructional photography by Mai Yong Vang of C&T Publishing, Inc., unless otherwise noted

Published by C&T Publishing, Inc., P.O. Box 1456, Lafayette, CA 94549

Library of Congress Cataloging-in-Publication Data

Names: Thomas, Donna Lynn, 1955- author.

Title: Teeny-tiny quilts : 35 miniature projects - tips & techniques for success / Donna Lynn Thomas.

Description: Lafayette, CA : C&T Publishing, Inc., 2018.

Identifiers: LCCN 2017044272 | ISBN 9781617456534 (soft cover)

Subjects: LCSH: Patchwork--Patterns. | Quilting--Patterns. | Miniature quilts.

Classification: LCC TT835 .T46355 2018 | DDC 746.46/041--dc23

LC record available at https://lccn.loc.gov/2017044272

Printed in the USA

10 9 8 7 6 5 4 3 2 1

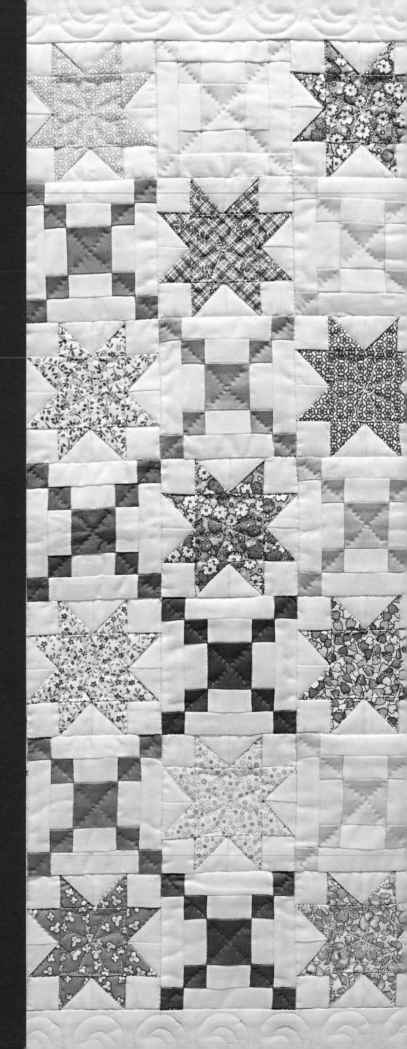

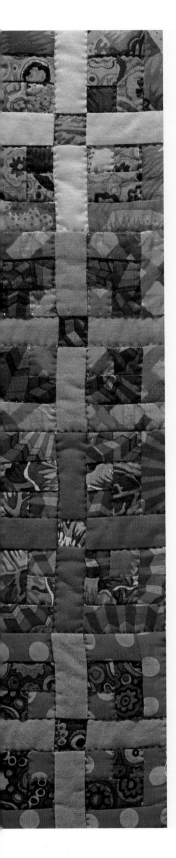

dedication

This book is dedicated to the love of my life, Terry Thomas, without whose loving support and devotion I could do nothing. We journey together always.

acknowledgments

A thousand, thousand *thank-yous* to all my friends and fellow quiltmakers who made samples, tested patterns, quilted, and offered advice when I needed to pick a brain. I can't thank you enough! You all worked on short notice and produced miracles. I am truly blessed to know so many lovely and talented quilters—and to call you all friends.

Kelly Ashton

Kath Brigham

Doris Brown

Ann Burgess

Jenise Cantlon

Barb Fife

Charlotte Freeman

Kari Hoyes

Denise Mariano

Linda Mooney

Beth Rhodes

Beth Woods

Many, many thanks to the two extremely talented women who quilt my quilts for me: Denise Mariano and Theresa Ward. Their work brings quilts to life, and they handled the demands of teeny, tiny quilts with amazing skill and creativity. Every trip to pick up a quilt had me filled with the anticipation of a child waiting for presents on Christmas morning.

And a special thank-you to Barb Eikmeier, who, although she didn't make a quilt, was always there to talk to and act as a sounding board. I can always count on her to provide sunshine, gentle encouragement, and sound guidance— along with good stories!

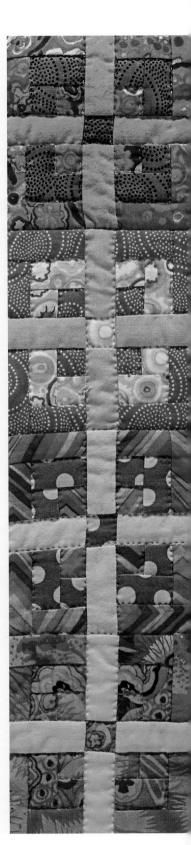

CONTENTS

THE QUILTS   40

INTRODUCTION

Primary Squares Smallest version with ¼″ finished size pieces. (Also see the *Primary Squares* project, page 47.)

Small things beckon us to come closer and take a look. So it is with small quilts. People feel compelled to pick them up, examine them, and wonder how someone could actually sew the tiny pieces together. And sewn they are—I don't paper piece.

I began making my first small quilts in the late 1970s when quilters still used templates. Unfortunately, one could go only so small before the templates were too tiny and hands too large to hold them. When I learned rotary cutting in 1985, it revolutionized my ability to make smaller and smaller quilts. I was hooked. There was joy in the challenge and the mastery of the skills. The tiniest of these quilts still make me giggle with each block because they are just so darned cute!

The upside to making small quilts, and not just the tiniest ones, is that when you return to your bigger blocks, they seem like dinosaurs. They practically put themselves together because you've mastered precision skills at a smaller scale.

I learned a lot about precision cutting and sewing by working with small quilts. So many things we take for granted now were new territory back then. Accurate rotary cutting rulers, a quilter's perfect ¼″ seam allowance, and pressing concepts were all things being discussed, designed, and figured out. I took all those new ideas and skills and applied them to miniature quilts, learning more on my own along the way.

There are very few things done differently with small quilts than with larger ones. They're just done with a bit more attention to detail. Most of the adjustments apply to only the smallest of the small.

I'll cover all those little tips, tricks, and skills in this book and provide a lot of opportunities to practice and hone your skills. I hope you enjoy diving into the world of small, smaller, and the smallest of quilts!

about this book

As you flipped through the pages of this book, you probably noticed a lot of sample quilts. In fact, there are 35 of them but only 12 patterns. Hmmm. Curious. Well, it seemed to me that it would be helpful to allow newcomers to ease gently into this new, small world in graduated increments rather than being thrown in headfirst.

Each pattern comes with two or three sizes—called **Small**, **Smaller**, and **Smallest**—and a sample for each of those sizes. Despite what you might think, the Small quilts are the larger versions in each pattern, with block sizes ranging from approximately 4″ to 6″. The next size down, Smaller quilts, have finished block sizes ranging from roughly 3″ to 4″. The Smallest are just that, with finished block sizes as small as 1⅛″ up to almost 3″.

In order to accommodate all this information in a book of less than 300 pages, you'll find a materials chart presented with each pattern, listing the fabric yardages for all the quilt sizes. Efficiently listing the cutting instructions was a little more challenging. The best solution was to create charts containing the cutting instructions for all the samples of that particular pattern.

The assembly instructions are written in a general way so as to apply to all the sizes in each pattern. That means the same assembly process and skills are used in exactly the same way for all sizes. For example, it is truly more difficult than it's worth—at least to me—to make a Flying Geese unit that is ⅜″ × ¾″ finished size using folded corners. (I'd rather eat a plateful of peas.) Instead, I pair two half-square triangle units together to make a *faux* Flying Geese unit. It's tons easier to make oversized half-square triangle units and trim them to a perfect size. Then, having pressed in such a way that diagonal seams nest, I sew them into pairs. Since all assembly instructions must be consistent for all sizes, there are no normal Flying Geese units in any quilts in this book, only the faux variety.

Not all the patterns have three samples. This is because not all the blocks would be feasible in all three sizes or else the largest block would extend past what I define as a Small block. Once a block reaches 6″, it's starting to pass that threshold, so you'll find only one 6″ block; the other Small blocks measure 5½″ or less. But you will find some really fun and small blocks to make!

Please be sure to read the information in Supplies (page 8) and Skills (page 13) before diving into the quilts themselves. The information on these pages is crucial to making tiny quilts. There are a lot of tips and tricks included, along with the basic and essential skills you should take the time to practice.

SUPPLIES

For the most part, with a few changes, you'll be using the same equipment and supplies as you do for your bigger quilts: sewing machine, rotary cutting equipment, iron, and ironing board.

sewing machine

You don't need a fancy machine to make pieced quilts, including miniatures. You *do* need a machine that sews a consistently high-quality straight seam without causing you to fuss with it to behave. Make sure your machine is cleaned and serviced and operating in tip-top condition, free from tension problems and other issues. If you have multiple machines, use your best for miniature quilts.

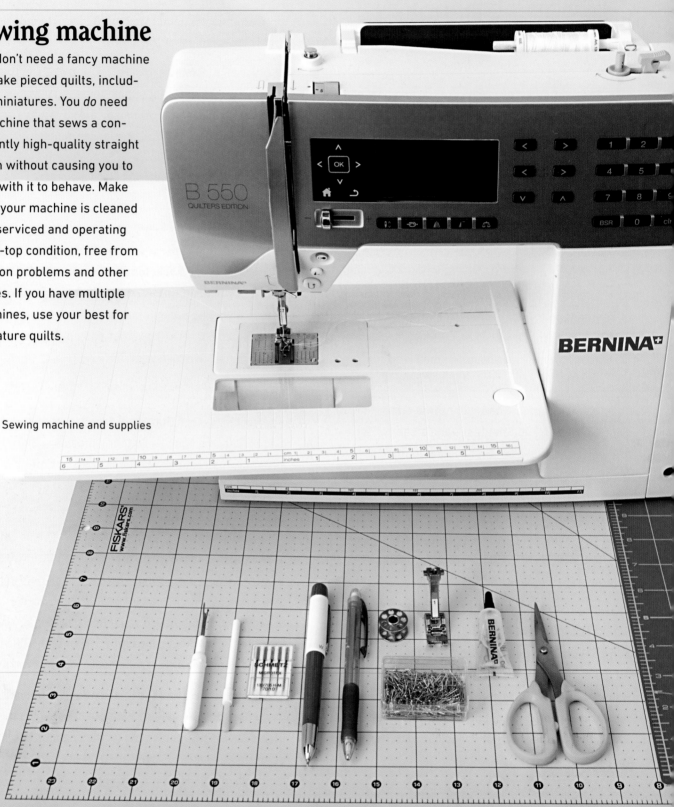

Sewing machine and supplies

Single-Stitch Throat Plate

Sometimes it's a good idea to invest in a single-stitch or straight-stitch throat plate. This is a plate with a small round hole for the needle to move up and down into the bobbin area. Your needle must be in the center position to use a single-stitch throat plate. The standard throat plate on most machines today has an oval hole that allows the needle to move sideways. For some machines, the oval hole provides the "opportunity" for your machine to pull down and eat your little pieces. That's not the case with all machines, so test your machine by sewing some small pieces and see how it reacts. Don't rush out and buy a single-stitch throat plate until you know how your machine handles small pieces. This is optional equipment.

Single-stitch throat plate

Presser Feet

The most important presser foot you need for piecing miniature quilts is your standard ¼″ seam allowance presser foot. It's also helpful to have the standard sewing presser foot on hand in case your guide isn't quite what it should be. I'll discuss more about presser feet later, when I cover seam allowances.

Needles

A lot of us don't even think about our sewing machine needles if all we do is piece. We buy universal #80 needles and call it good.

With small seams it's important to sew a fine seam using finer needles. A sharps needle, such as microtex #70 needle (by Schmetz), will help provide that finer seam. Fine sharp needles are less likely to push points and pieces down into the bobbin area or mangle the start of a seam as larger universal needles can do on occasion.

Change your needle frequently, after every eight to ten hours of sewing. If you hear a popping noise with each stitch, you waited too long to change your needle. A dull, bent, or burred needle can cause damage to your machine as well as break your thread or sew bad stitches.

rotary cutting equipment

Cutters

Standard 45 mm cutters are just fine for the Small quilts in this book. When you start getting to the Smaller and Smallest sizes, a smaller cutter is more maneuverable than the larger ones. There are two sizes smaller than the 45 mm: the 28 mm and the 18 mm. I'll leave the choice up to you. I use both interchangeably.

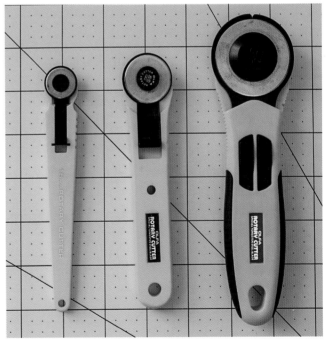

Three sizes of rotary cutters suitable for small quilts

Mats

Rotary cutting mats are designed to be used with rotary cutters. Look for a self-healing mat with or without marked grid lines. You won't be using the gridlines for precision cutting, and their wide line spacing means they aren't useful for miniature work.

An 18″ × 24″ mat is perfectly adequate for these quilts, and the 12″ × 18″ mat is all you need for the smallest quilts. A lot of our fabric "yardages" are small or scrap size, and you don't need a large mat to accommodate them.

Rulers

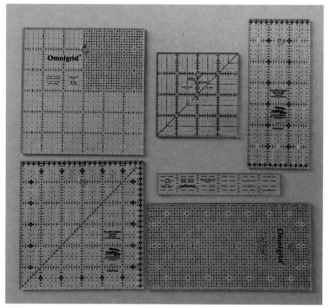

Useful rulers for miniature quiltmaking

Good ⅛″-thick acrylic rulers with detailed markings are essential for cutting the pieces required for small and miniature quilts. This also means more ruler lines and markings, which can take getting used to for some quilters. Be assured that the extra lines are essential when cutting or truing up pieces that measure less than an inch. With practice, you'll grow to appreciate the precision in detailed lines.

Generally, you want a ruler with an ⅛″ allover grid or close to it. The lines should be fine with numerous "windows" along the inch and half-inch intersections. Use the windows to align your fabric edges with the ruler lines for accurate cutting.

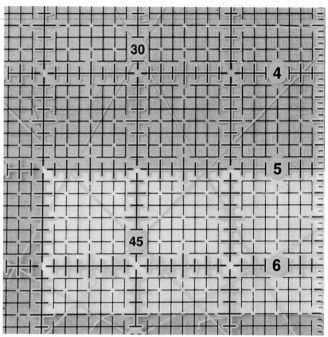

Use the "windows" between marks to line up the edges of your fabric.

For cutting larger pieces, you need a ruler that's about 3″–4″ wide and about 12″–14″ long.

You also need a second, smaller ruler with similar markings for closer work, such as cutting segments and trimming seam allowances.

The third essential ruler is a 4″–6″ square-up ruler with a line running across one diagonal. Use this for trimming half-square triangle units and squaring up patches and blocks as you sew.

A 1″ × 6″ or 1″ × 8″ ruler is helpful for measuring strip tests and measuring the accuracy of what you've sewn as you work. I have one right next to me whenever I am sewing.

threads

To achieve a fine seam, you need a fine thread. The thicker the thread, the more room it takes up in the seam, thus cutting back on the finished size of your pieces. This is a minuscule consideration on larger piecing, but on a small scale, it matters.

It's best to use 100% cotton thread. You can successfully use all kinds of beautiful synthetic threads for your surface stitching such as quilting, decorative stitching, and embellishments. But when it comes to seams, you want your thread to be strong but not stronger than the cotton fabric we are sewing.

Think about it this way. Synthetic threads are much stronger than the cotton yarns in fabric.

A seam under stress is going to give in one of two places: Either the thread is going to break or the fabric will tear to release the stress. If the thread is stronger than the fabric, the fabric will tear. If the thread is weaker than the fabric, the fabric will stay intact as the thread breaks first. You can replace the thread in a seam, but torn fabric will never be the same.

Choose fine 50-weight or preferably 60-weight, long-staple Egyptian cotton thread; the larger the weight number, the finer the thread. For example, 60-weight is finer than 50-weight. Aurifil now sells an 80-weight cotton thread. With so many good quality cotton threads available, try different ones and choose what you like best as long as it is 50-weight or (preferably) finer.

Use neutral colors that will blend with the colors of your fabrics. Unlike garment sewing and appliqué, you won't try to match colors when piecing. The rule of thumb is the thread should not be lighter than the lightest fabric or darker than the darkest. Shades of gray, cream, or tan will be your most frequent choices of sewing thread color.

ironing supplies

Ironing equipment doesn't need to be fancy, but there are a few features to look for and some to avoid. The essentials are a clean ironing surface, a clean iron with a cotton setting, and some ironing sprays.

The Iron

Irons come in a wide array of styles with features galore. All that's needed is a good, clean iron that heats to a cotton setting. In fact, steam or spray capabilities aren't essential either. The truth is that steam is overrated as a desirable feature for pressing pieced patches and blocks. A spray bottle of water is preferable.

The holes in the soleplate that allow for steam to escape are also prone to gathering up the tiny points of smaller pieces and mangling them beyond repair. I also find that when using a normal size iron, my little pieces frequently get stuck to the soleplate and are scorched if not removed quickly.

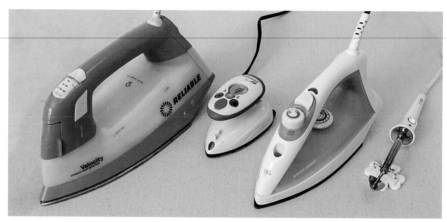

Irons come in all shapes and sizes with assorted bells and whistles.

For the Smaller and Smallest block sizes, a travel or craft iron is most useful, especially when used dry. There are quite a variety of good ones available.

No matter which iron you use, keep the soleplate clean and free from chemical build-up if you use sprays or adhesives. Remember to turn it off when you are done sewing.

Ironing Surfaces

The most important feature is a firm surface, not a soft one. A firm surface enables crisp seams. Be sure to keep your surface clean, and replace it if it is worn out, torn, scorched, or embedded with too many chemicals.

Sprays

It's best to press most seams with a dry iron to avoid stretching. Unfortunately, more often than not, a dry iron leaves a softly rolled seam as opposed to the nice, crisp, fully pressed seam you'll need. To get that sharp crease, spray the rolled seam with water and then press again without moving the iron in any direction other than up and down. You'll need a good spray bottle that will send out a misty spray as opposed to streams of water.

Best Press and spray water help remove wrinkles and make sharp creases in seams.

Some quilters like to starch their fabrics, especially when working with small and mini quilts. I'm not a fan of heavy starch but the light linen variety is fine. I prefer Mary Ellen's Best Press, a spray alternative, which does an excellent job of removing stubborn wrinkles and creates sharp seams in the most stubborn of fabrics without leaving flakes or starch buildup.

SKILLS

For this book, it's assumed that you have mastered basic rotary cutting and machine piecing skills. The following skills are helpful tips and tricks that make the process more accurate and enjoyable.

choosing fabrics

It's always exciting to pick fabrics for a new quilt project. Although you will generally follow the same principles when choosing fabrics for miniature quilts as you do for larger quilts, there are a few special considerations to keep in mind when working with smaller quilts.

Stick with tightly woven 100% cottons. Synthetics can be slippery and difficult to control. Shot cottons and small woven checks and plaids can add charm to your quilts, but be sure they aren't too heavy for the scale of the quilt or unravel too easily.

When working with the Smaller and Smallest quilts, you want to use a variety of types of prints, including paisleys, large and small florals, stripes, checks, small prints, dots, and solids, just as you would with a large quilt. But it's very important to keep in mind the scale of the print in relation to the quilt. Many prints that would be considered small or medium-small on a large bed quilt would be appropriate as a large print for a small quilt. Conversely, most very large or widely spaced prints don't work well with minis. It's all about scale.

Here are some good choices of fabrics for smaller quilts. Notice the variety of types of prints included in the collection.

All these prints are appropriate for Smaller and Smallest quilts.

I stumbled onto another issue years ago when I first started making miniature quilts. The three small prints (below) seem to be perfect for a miniature quilt, right?... Not quite. They are each wonderful for mini quilts but not so much when used with other multicolor or similarly colored prints as in this little Ohio Star block. Look closely at the triangle points and edges where the color in one print meets up with the same color in an adjacent print. The star points and seam edges can "bleed out" and disappear.

It's not too bad on this block (below), but it can be far worse if you're not careful. Try to use monochromatic prints, and if using a multicolor print, don't place it next to a print that's the same color as one in the multicolor print. The same thing happens on big blocks, but you don't notice it because there's plenty of space for your eyes and brain to connect the seamlines for you. But on the small seams and points of tiny blocks, it just isn't possible and the points are lost.

Be careful to choose prints that won't bleed into another print with similar colors.

These small multicolor prints seem perfect for a miniature quilt but can cause problems if you're not careful.

Be careful of the use of contrast in miniatures. Contrast is created through the use of value, the degree of dark and light between prints, the scale of prints used in the quilt, and the use of different colors. It's fun to use subtle value gradations or low-contrast soft pastels on big quilts. Unfortunately, such subtlety is lost on a small quilt because the eye blends it all together into a form-less mush the farther away you move from the quilt.

Look at what happens to the two basket blocks (below). From the distance, the second small basket with higher contrast is less subtle but much more effective than the low-value version. Low-value differences are fun to play with on a big block, but the pattern of a small block is lost without sharper contrasts.

Although this Philadelphia Cobblestone block employs good dark and light contrast, the two prints are both busy, causing a bit of visual chaos. There isn't anywhere for the eye to rest, and it's harder to identify the pattern. The block would work better if one or both of the prints were calmer.

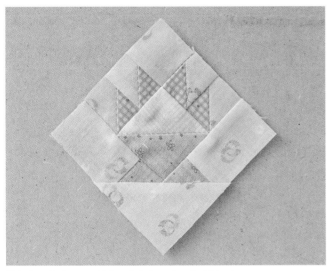

Subtlety is lost on this miniature basket block.

Two very busy prints can be chaotic sitting next to each other in a small quilt block.

Stronger use of value works better on little blocks.

This block is much easier to look at because the prints are calmer.

Another issue to consider is the use of too many busy fabrics together. On big blocks, your eye visually distinguishes between patterns over the length of a seam. With the smallest quilts, there isn't enough seam length for your eye to do so and you lose the pattern definition if you're not careful.

The bottom line is you have to employ sharper value and color contrast in the fabric choices for the smallest of quilts.

cutting

Cutting the pieces for miniature quilts is no different than cutting for larger quilts. Precision is the keyword in all instances. Since the pieces for mini quilts are much smaller, you need more detail on your rulers to achieve the necessary precision.

Please don't use mat lines to measure for cutting quilts, as they don't have the necessary ⅛″ grids. Additionally, the grid lines they do have are too thick and can wear off or become grooved and inaccurate. You must use your ruler, measuring from the edge of your fabric.

Since most small quilts are cut from smaller chunks of fabric, such as fat quarters, fat eighths, 10″ squares, or remnants, you'll rarely be cutting full-length 40″ strips. Even so, it's still convenient to fold your 20″-wide fabric pieces into two layers, aligning the selvage with the opposite edge and cutting perpendicular to the fold.

NOTE
The farther you stretch to cut, the less power and control you may have and the more opportunity there is for the ruler to shift or for you to lose accurate control of the ruler or cutter. Folding your fabric into layers helps reduce how far you reach to cut. It also keeps the smaller ruler markings within better range of your eyes. Additionally, short people, like myself, simply don't have the physical reach to accurately cut across large spans of fabric.

sewing

The general process for sewing small blocks is the same as for any piecing. There are a few extra things you can do to increase the accuracy of your piecing, which is critical in ensuring your blocks fit together well.

The Perfect ¼″ Seam Allowance

When piecing quilts, sew with an accurate ¼″ seam allowance. The dimensions for the seam allowances are built into the pieces you cut. Sew seams from raw edge to raw edge without backstitching at the beginning or end of a seam.

The most important gift you can give yourself is the mastery of a perfect ¼″ seam. Quilt blocks are similar to jigsaw puzzles. If the pieces aren't the size they're supposed to be, nothing is going to fit right and you'll feel more frustration than pleasure in the process. When working with small quilts and small pieces, it's even more important to sew an accurate ¼″ seam allowance, as there's no room for small errors.

Most sewing machine companies make a special ¼″ presser foot just for quiltmaking. It's very important that you check the accuracy of that guide and make sure you're using it correctly.

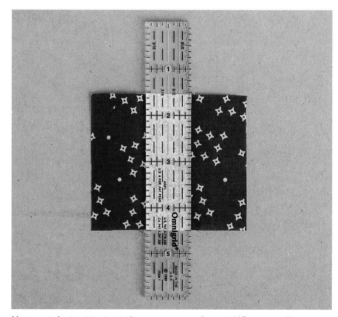

Use a strip test to test the accuracy of your ¼″ seam allowance.

1 Conduct a strip test by cutting 3 strips precisely 1½″ wide by about 3″ long.

2 Sew them together side by side, using your best skills to align the strip edges perfectly.

3 Sew slowly and carefully with a consistent ¼″ seam, following the guide for your machine.

4 When you're done, finger-press the seams away from the center strip. Place a 1″-wide ruler onto the middle strip. It should slide onto the center strip in between the seam ridges without stretching to make it fit. Conversely, there shouldn't be any room for it to shift from side to side either.

If your center strip measures a perfect 1″ wide, you are clear to sew. If not, you need to do a little detective work to understand what's wrong and how to fix it.

If the center strip is too narrow, your seam allowance is too wide. If the center strip is too wide, your seam allowance is too narrow. The question is why. The problem can be the guide, you, or the ability of the two of you to work well together. Examine your strip test in light of the possible issues listed below. Once you find the problem or problems, make the necessary corrections and repeat the strip test until you can produce a perfect 1″ center strip several times in a row.

- Check the cut size of the strips just in case the problem is there.

- Look at the raw edges of the seams. Were they truly well aligned or are there some parts of the edges that don't match up perfectly?

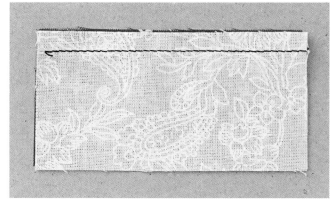

Raw edges not accurately or consistently aligned

- Is the stitching on both seams the same consistent width from start to finish? This is often the problem.

Inconsistent seam width stitching

- When you sew, are the fabric edges sticking out past the presser foot or other ¼″ guide even just a bit? Or in reverse, are they hidden too far under the presser foot? Neither scenario is desirable. The fabric should perfectly align with the edge of the guide or presser foot.

You shouldn't see any fabric edges to the right of the presser foot.

If all these things are good but the center strip still isn't right, then the problem may be with the guide itself. This can be remedied by shifting the needle position a bit to the right to make a narrower seam or to the left to make a wider seam. Don't use a single-stitch throat plate if you're moving the needle to the left or right. Test each needle position until you find the one that produces a perfect 1″-wide center strip. Write down the setting so you don't forget what you learned.

If you can't shift the needle position, you can create a guide for yourself using graph paper.

1 Carefully cut an accurate 1″ × 3″ strip of graph paper.

2 Place the strip under your unthreaded machine needle.

3 Lower the needle into the first ¼″ line from the right edge of the paper.

4 Arrange the paper so it is running straight from front to back and not tilted to either side. Place a piece of painter's tape next to the right edge.

5 Remove the paper and test the accuracy of this guide. Adjust the tape slightly as needed until you are able to consistently produce a perfect strip test. Once you have found the perfect position, you can build up the tape with multiple layers or use a product such as Sewing Edge—Reusable Vinyl Stops for Your Machine (by C&T Publishing) or Seam Guide (by Guidelines4Quilting) to provide a ridge to run your pieces against.

There are several guides available on the market that attach to your sewing machine worktable and provide perfect seamlines as well as perform other tasks. One of my favorites is Clearly Perfect Angles (by New Leaf Stitches).

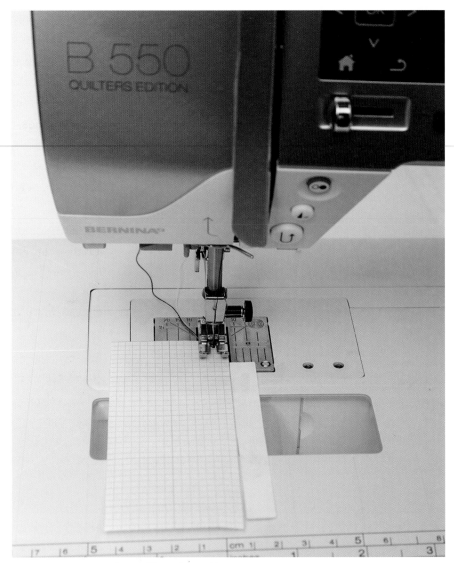

Use graph paper to find a ¼″ sewing guide.

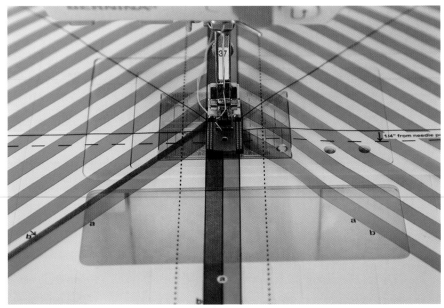

Use a purchased sewing guide to master the ¼″ seam allowance.

Machine Settings

There are a few adjustments to make to your sewing machine settings to accommodate the sizes associated with small and miniature quiltmaking.

Stitch length   The stitch length for routine sewing is about eight to ten stitches per inch. Most new machines use numbers ranging from zero to five instead of the old stitches per inch measure. If your little bitty seams are only ⅜″–½″ finished size, with a routine stitch length, there would be only three or four stitches across the full length of the seam. That's not enough to secure the seam, so you want to shorten your stitch length. Since machines have different ways of numbering, shorten your stitch length until you measure about fifteen stitches per inch using a ruler. You don't want the stitches so tight that you can't remove them when necessary.

Needle position   Set your machine or make it a habit to always stop with your needle down in fabric such as scrap leads. The practical reason is that the machine's take-up lever will not be able to unthread your needle when you start sewing. It also helps you create the habit of sewing with scraps. For more on this, see Scrap Leads (page 20).

Stitching speed   Come on and admit it. You like to sew fast! Well, that's not generally a good thing. You lose control at high speeds, and these seams are so short you can be across them—*badly*—in the blink of an eye if you're going too fast. Engage your speed control if you have one. If not, pay careful attention to sewing slowly. The seams are short, so it doesn't take long to sew them at a slower speed.

Presser foot pressure   This is probably not something you think about routinely, but it is something that can affect the quality of your piecing. The presser foot has to press down with adequate pressure to keep the fabric pieces securely together when they are being sewn. But if the pressure is too great, it can shove the top layer ahead of the bottom layer. This can cause intersections to shift out of alignment, make it difficult for the machine to hold bias edges together and stable, and even make it difficult to handle the edges of anything you're sewing.

If while sewing, you notice either your top layer rippling ahead of the presser foot, your bias edges not aligning when you sew them, or your having to pin all intersections to keep them aligned, the problem may be there is too much pressure from your presser foot. Many new machines, especially those able to embroider, give you the ability to adjust the pressure, in which case you may want to try lightening the pressure a bit until the problems go away. If that doesn't work or you have a machine that does not allow adjustments, take the machine to your service technician and let them adjust it if they can. Take samples of your problems and bring fabric so you can demonstrate what is going on.

Chain Sewing

Chain sewing applies an assembly line approach to the sewing process. When piecing, sew all the same seams together one right after the other until all like seams are sewn. Repeat with the next set of seams until you have nothing left to sew without having to stop and press.

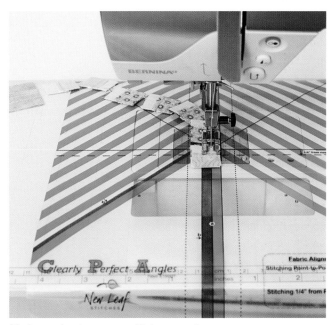

Chain sewing improves efficiency and accuracy.

One of the benefits of chain sewing, aside from increased efficiency and speed, is memory learning. You learn and master new things by repeating them over and over until the memory sticks. With each repeat of the same seam or sequence, you refine and improve your technique. Chain sewing is a good memory tool and skill builder.

Scrap Leads

Many machines have little quirks. Sewing across a set of scraps can help alleviate quite a few of those quirks. I started using scrap leads back in the mid-1980s and have taught their benefits ever since. So what are scrap leads and why would you use them?

Scrap leads are two small strips of fabric the same weight as what you're sewing. For quilters, that means two strips of cotton. Begin any stretch of sewing by stitching across a pair of strips from the back right up to the front of the strips, stopping with your needle down in the front edge of the scraps. *Don't lift your presser foot or remove the strips.* You're now ready to start sewing your quilt strips or pieces.

With the scrap leads intact, chain sew as many seams as you can at one time. End by sewing across a second set of scrap strips, stopping with your needle down in the front of them. Again, *don't lift your presser foot or remove the strips.* Cut the kite-tail of piecing off the back edge of the scraps and you're ready to start stitching again without a loose thread tail in sight!

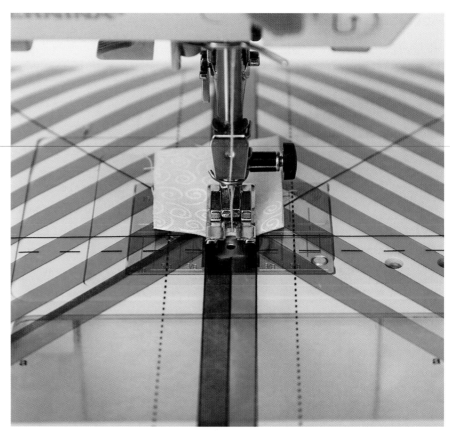

Start all new sewing with a set of scraps.

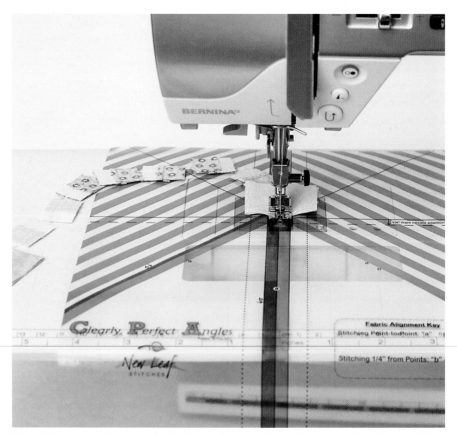

Stop with your needle down in the front of a second set of scraps and you're ready to start sewing again.

Why does this work?

My first sewing machine, like some today, had a tendency to pull everything off to the left as it fed out the back of the presser foot. This would distort the first part of the seam so it wasn't consistently straight from the start. But if the back of the presser foot and feed dogs were already engaged with the scrap leads when the seams to be sewn came under the front, the pull stopped. As a result, scrap leads ensured that the seam was good along its entire length.

Some machines sew a few rough first stitches and then calm down and sew beautifully. If you are using scraps, those rough stitches occur on the scraps, not your good seam. With the short seams in miniature quilts, you can't afford to have any rough stitches.

Some machines require you to hold the thread tails when you first start stitching. If you don't, they create a bird's nest of thread at the start of the seam. These quirks are absorbed onto the scrap leads, and as long as you keep scrap leads in place all the time, you won't have to deal with the bird's nesting again. There's no room for thread wads on the short seams of miniature piecing.

Some machines, especially those with wide openings for side-to-side motion stitching, will suck down points and small pieces into the bobbin area, eat them up, and sometimes not give them back. With scrap leads, the opening on the throat plate is covered, making it impossible for anything to be pulled down below.

The one thing that affects everyone is thread waste. Each thread tail is thread wasted. Scrap leads cut down on thread waste. Good quality thread is too expensive to be careless with it.

The Better Finger

Often with miniatures, fingers are too big to keep control of little pieces as they're guided under the presser foot. Try using a stiletto, seam ripper, or other pointy tool to do the job for you. It will hold intersections together with pinpoint accuracy and allow you to make minute adjustments in the pieces and layers as

you sew. You'll have a lighter and more accurate touch and, if using a seam ripper, it's right there to slice the thread twists connecting your piecing to the scrap leads when you're done sewing. I've been sewing with a seam ripper in my hand for more than 30 years. Give it a try. With a little practice, you'll find it one of the handiest little tips for all your piecing.

Use a sharp pointy tool as a Better Finger.

Taming the Triangle

We quilters have developed many techniques to avoid sewing the bias edges of half-square triangles.

The bias grain on the long edges of the triangles stretches very easily. The key to success with bias is to be aware of where it is and avoid doing things that encourage it to stretch. The most important of these are rough handling and moisture. Both send bias edges into a tizzy.

Here are instructions, including a few tips and trouble-shooting suggestions, to take away the fear of sewing triangles and any other bias seam.

1 Always begin by sewing across a set of scrap leads and stop with the needle down in the front of the scraps.

2 Align your triangles right sides together. Lift the presser foot and place the tips of the triangles directly on the scrap leads so they are protected from being sucked down into the bowels of the bobbin area, never to be seen again. Leave enough space for one or two stitches between the triangles and the scraps. Put the presser foot down and begin stitching slowly.

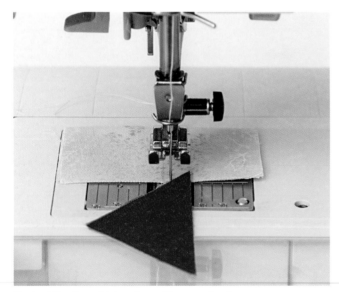

Protect the tips of triangles with scrap leads.

3 When sewing, use a very light touch and let the feed dogs and presser foot do their jobs. If you hold onto the pieces or put the weight of your hands on them as you sew, you're exerting resistance against the feed dogs, which are pulling the fabric under the presser foot and out the back. Stretching is likely to occur.

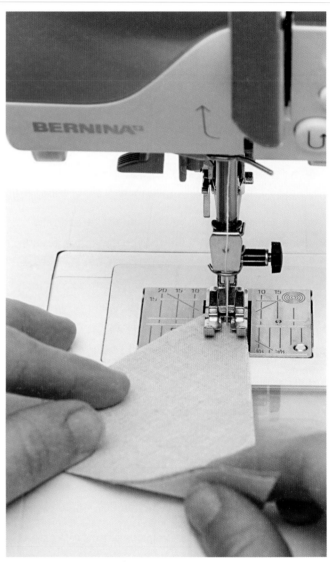

Over-handling bias edges can stretch them.

4 Sew slowly. Bias edges can be hard to keep aligned if you sew too fast.

5 Use your Better Finger to keep everything under control.

6 If you notice your machine has trouble keeping the bias aligned and the pieces seem to want to separate, stop. There are a couple of solutions.

a. The first is to check presser foot pressure. Sometimes, if it's too strong, it will force the top piece in the seam forward a bit and shift sideways. Adjust the pressure.

b. Some machines with wide feed dogs have trouble keeping bias edges aligned when the feed dogs are not completely covered by the presser foot. Replace the narrower ¼″ foot with the wider standard presser foot that better covers the feed dogs. Shift the needle position to the right until it sews a perfect ¼″ seam. Be sure to use strip tests to assess this.

If you find the exposed feed dogs causing problems, use a wider foot that covers them.

7 When you reach the end of the seam, stop with your needle down in the edge of the pieces. Lift your presser foot slightly and place the tips of the next triangle pair on top of the tips of the ones you just sewed. It's a heck of a machine that can suck down four layers of fabric.

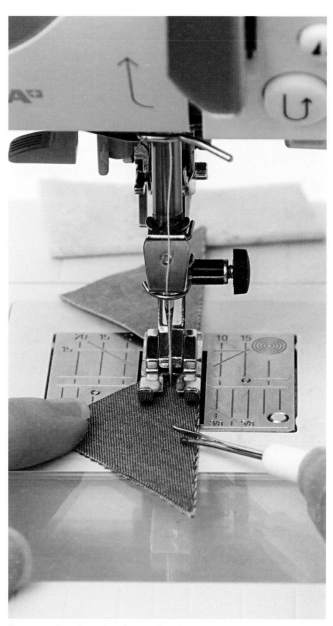

Protect triangle points by putting the tips on top of the tips of the previous pair.

Continue in this fashion to sew all your triangle pairs or other bias seams, protecting points as you go.

Nesting Seams

When you make quilt blocks, you start with individual pieces and sew them into pieced patches. Then you join the patches into rows and finally sew the rows together to complete a block. Where seams from one pieced unit line up with the seams from another pieced unit you want the corners to match and points to be sharp. You also want the seam allowances to be disbursed in such a way that the block lays flat and seam allowances aren't piled on top of seam allowances, causing unsightly bulkiness.

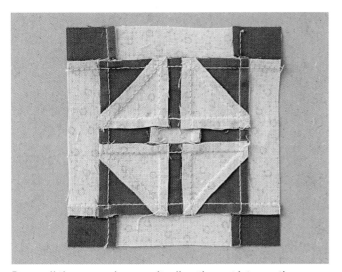

Press all the seams in opposite directions at intersections.

To that end, you will use a process called *nesting seams*. It is of primary importance in ensuring sharp points and flat blocks. The idea is to press all seams that will meet at an intersection in opposite directions so the ridges of the two seam allowances snuggle up tightly next to each other at the intersection. It becomes even more critical with small and miniature blocks as small discrepancies are more noticeable.

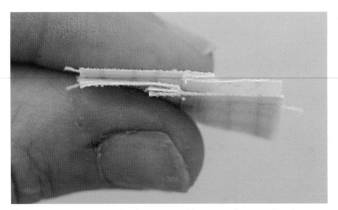

To nest seams, snuggle the seam ridges against each other.

By nesting seams, you can dispense with pinning intersections. When pins are pulled out of position in order to sew across an intersection, the pieces are pulled slightly out of alignment, making a mess of miniature intersections.

It's important to nest all straight seams as well as diagonal seams whenever they meet other seams.

Nest seams that meet perpendicular to the seam.

Nest seams that meet at an angle.

When two diagonals meet at one or both ends of a seam, it's critical to make sure they are nesting. Once nested, start sewing from the end of the seam where they meet to lock in a sharp point.

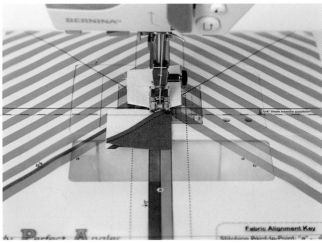

Begin sewing at the corner where the seams form a point.

When sewing together segments or pieced rows that are nested, try sewing them so the seam on the top layer is facing *toward* the needle instead of away.

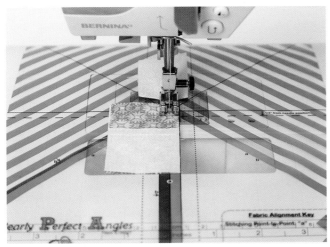

To avoid gaps at intersections, sew with the seam allowance facing the needle whenever you can.

You don't always have this choice, but when you do, face the seam on the top layer toward the needle. The instinct is to face it away from the needle, thinking the presser foot will glide over the intersection more easily. While this may be true, it can also push the top layer away from the needle slightly and thus away from the intersection, causing misalignment.

When the seam faces away from the needle, sometimes the intersection can be pushed out of alignment.

If the top seams are facing the needle, the ridge of the opposing seams on the bottom will automatically stop the top ridge from moving out of alignment. In fact, it forces it into a nice tight match.

Sometimes there's no perfect pressing solution. In that case, if it will help, I commit quilting heresy and press one end of a seam in one direction and the other end in the opposite direction so that both ends nest at their respective intersections. A little snip in the middle of the seam allowance and some spray will help the seam flip in the middle. Nesting is that important.

Sometimes it's necessary to flip one end of a seam in one direction and the other end in a different direction.

Sewing Across the X

When sewing rows and blocks, you often come across an intersection where a straight seam intersects a diagonal seam forming an X. When possible you want to sew with the X intersection on the top so you can see it clearly when sewing the next seam.

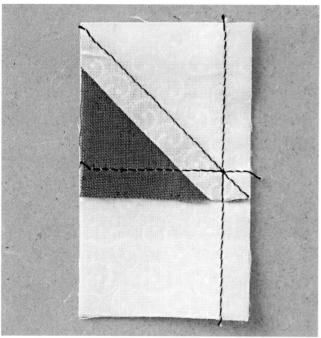

Sew with the X intersection on top where it can be seen.

Begin by tightly nesting any seam ridges involved. While sewing, make sure your stitching line crosses right through the X created by the intersection. Once sewn, check the right side to make sure you've hit the mark perfectly. A thread or two off will end in lopped off points on the right side. Adjust if necessary.

If sewn correctly, there will be a nice sharp point on the front.

Point-to-Point Sewing

A great deal of care is needed when sewing small pieced rows and units together. Zipping across the seam doesn't work well because you lose control of the intersections in the blink of an eye. The best approach is to follow these steps, always beginning with a scrap lead.

1 Nest the first intersection and, securing it with the Better Finger, stitch up to the intersection, stopping with the needle down one stitch past it.

2 Using the Better Finger, adjust the next intersection, hold it securely, and stitch across it, again stopping with the needle down a stitch past the intersection.

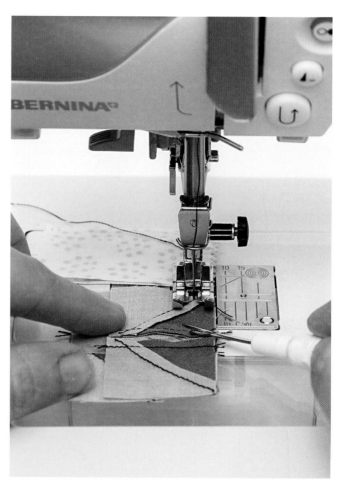

Stitch intricate seams from intersection to intersection.

3 Continue across all the intersections, stitching slowly from one to the next to the next until the seam is completely sewn. Stop with your needle down in the end of the seam.

4 Chain sew more seams or end with a scrap lead.

Controlling Seam Bounce

Seam bounce is a funky little phenomenon you run into when you're working on very small block piecing. It happens when you're sewing blocks and rows together and the fabric from the previously sewn seam is close to or just under the left edge of the presser foot. The ridge and bulk of the seam allowance cause the presser foot to bounce or be pushed to the right, completely ruining the seam you're trying to sew.

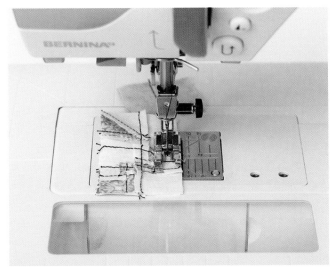

Sometimes the presser foot gets bumped by the narrower piecing and seams along its left edge.

To control this, slide a laminated or glossy postcard over the bulk of the previously sewn seam and just under the left edge of the presser foot. This allows the presser foot to glide over the seam and not be bounced to the right.

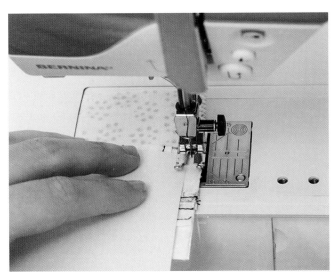

Use a laminated postcard to alleviate seam bounce.

Trimming Seams

Although you sew all seams ¼″ wide no matter the size of the block, you need to trim them to ⅛″ on the Smallest blocks. Any block that's 3″ or less or composed of pieces smaller than ¾″ finished size should have its seams trimmed to ⅛″.

There are advantages to staying with a ¼″ seam instead of trying to sew a ⅛″ seam. The math for figuring cut sizes is the same, and you have larger pieces to hold onto with a regular ¼″ seam than if you cut and sewed them using the smaller seam allowance.

Before you do any trimming, carefully check your piecing to make sure it is correctly done. Make sure the pieces measure the right sizes and are oriented in the correct position. Once you've trimmed the seams, it's very difficult to fix any errors.

Trim the seams by placing the ⅛″ mark of your ruler on the stitching line. Trim the seams. I call the remains quilt dust.

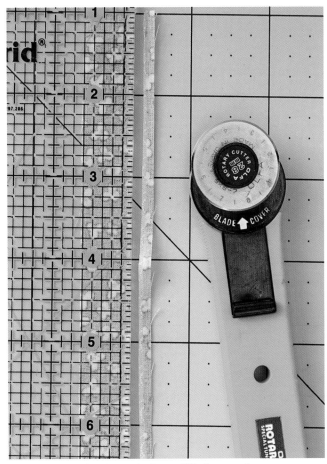

Trim seams of Smallest piecing to ⅛″ after sewing.

Making Half-Square Triangle Units

For the sake of accuracy, all half-square triangle units in this book are cut and sewn oversized and trimmed to the correct size. I added 1″ instead of ⅞″ to the finished size of the short leg to create slightly oversized half-square triangles. To square up the sewn units, use a square ruler with a diagonal line running across it from corner to corner. The measurements on the sides adjacent to the diagonal line should come in to meet it, forming squares of assorted sizes in ⅛″ increments.

Follow these instructions for sewing accurate half-square triangle units. As an example, let's say you want to make ½″ finished size half-square triangle units. Add 1″ to finished size and cut 1½″ squares from each print. Cut the squares once diagonally. After sewing you'll need to trim the finished units to 1″ (½″ finished size plus ½″ for seam allowances).

1 Sew 2 half-square triangles together on their long edges (see Taming the Triangle, page 22).

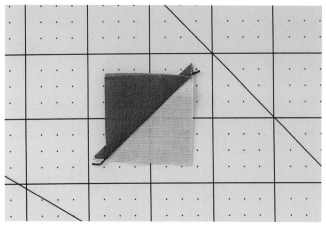

Oversized half-square triangle unit

2 Press them carefully in the direction indicated in the pattern (see Pressing Bias Seams, page 30).

3 Using the square-up ruler, lay the diagonal line on the seam as in the diagram. Arrange the ruler so the 1″ measurements are just inside the raw edges underneath the ruler. Make sure there is excess fabric sticking out beyond the ruler edges on the top corners as well.

4 Trim the top 2 edges.

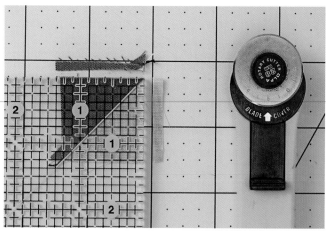

Trim top two edges.

5 Turn the unit around so the freshly cut edges are closest to you. Place the diagonal line of the ruler back on the seam with the 1″ measurements aligned precisely on the cut edges near you. The excess of the last 2 sides will stick out past the corner of the ruler as before. Trim the last 2 sides.

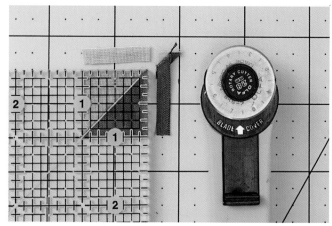

Turn and trim bottom two edges.

You now have a perfectly sized half-square triangle unit even if there were a few discrepancies when you sewed and pressed. Repeat this process for each half-square triangle unit.

pressing

Pressing seams is as important as cutting and sewing, especially when it comes to miniature quilts. Always press your yardage or fabric pieces smooth and wrinkle-free using steam and sprays as necessary. Proper pressing also ensures that your seams are crisp, straight, and will nest together well.

Pressing Seams

The goal of pressing seams is twofold. First is to ensure that the bulk of the seam allowances is disbursed evenly at intersections. The second is to ensure that all seams meeting at an intersection nest together, forming tight corners and points without the use of pins as much as possible. These two goals are interdependent.

All seam-pressing instructions in this book are indicated by arrows in each diagram, showing which direction to press the seams sewn in that step.

A well-pressed seam is straight, pressed cleanly and smoothly to one side, and without any puckers, distortions, or tension problems. Here are the instructions for successful pressing.

1 Use a clean, dry iron on the cotton setting. Steam can distort seams, so only use it after the seam is pressed in place.

2 Set the seam first. Press the seam flat before pressing it to one side or the other. This helps the thread relax into the weave of the fabric a bit, making for a much smoother and finer turn. It can also help alleviate any *small* tension problems with the thread. Serious tension problems need to be dealt with by you or a service technician.

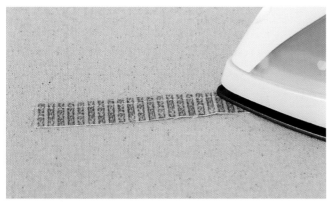

Set the seam first.

3 Place the fabric with the side to which the seam is to be pressed on the top.

4 Working from the top, use the tip of the iron to nudge the top layer of fabric over the seam allowance, which is held in place on the ironing board. Use gentle, not aggressive, motions being aware of where the bias grain is to avoid pressing into it and stretching it.

Place with fabric toward which you want the seam pressed on top. Press seams to one side.

5 Once the seam is pressed in place, you can spray it with water or Best Press to make a sharp crease. At this point use only an up and down motion with the iron.

6 Always press each seam in a strip set before attaching more strips to it, especially with small and miniature quilts, they easily become an unmanageable tangle of strips that's difficult to press without stretching or distorting them.

NOTE

Always press from the front; trying to press seam allowances from the back often produces small pleats in the seam, resulting in inaccuracies and future piecing problems.

Pressing Bias Seams

Seams with the bias grain along the seam must be treated carefully to avoid stretching. Avoid moisture and harsh motions when pressing them. Instead, gently nudge the iron in the direction of the straight grain.

This is especially important with half-square triangles. Most of us have a tendency to use the tip of the iron to flip open the triangle and press into it. This can be the cause of serious stretching and distortion.

Press bias-edged seams by moving the iron in the direction of the straight grain.

The Four-Patch Pop

Sometimes you will want the seams in a four-patch unit or block to spin in a circular direction. By pressing this way, the seams are well disbursed and the center flat and perfectly matched.

There's a simple little trick that makes this easy to do.

1 When you look at the back of the four-patch (at right) you can see the vertical top and bottom seams are pressed in opposite directions. The final center seam is running horizontally. In order for the seams to flow in a circular fashion, the two halves of the final seam need to flip in different directions. The left side needs to flip up and the right side down.

Sometimes you'll want the seams in a four-patch unit to flow in a circular direction.

2 Here's how to do this: With your right thumb and hand, hold the right side of the seam down about halfway between the right side and the center intersection.

3 With your left thumb and hand, hold the left side of the seam up at the halfway point between the side and the center.

Pop the center intersection so seams flow in a circular direction.

4 Now all at one time give a sharp little twist down with your right hand and a sharp twist up with the left hand. The seam will pop into place. This is called the *four-patch pop*. It works like a charm unless you're trying to press seams in the wrong direction or are using a microscopic stitch length.

The four-patch pop produces seams that flow in a circular direction.

FINISHING MINIATURE QUILTS

There isn't a lot that's different about assembling miniature quilts compared with big quilts. Sometimes you'll use sashings, alternate one or two blocks together in a quilt, set blocks straight or on the diagonal, and add plain or pieced borders as desired. You'll layer, baste, and bind the quilts pretty much like bigger quilts. Still there are a few tips or changes to observe when finishing them, particularly the smallest ones.

sashings

Sashings are strips of fabric that join blocks together. They can be sewn together with sashing squares or without.

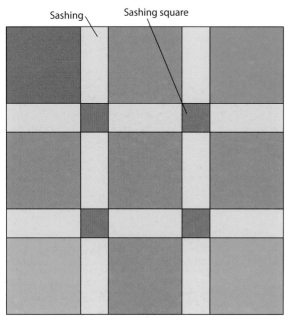

A quilt with sashing and sashing squares

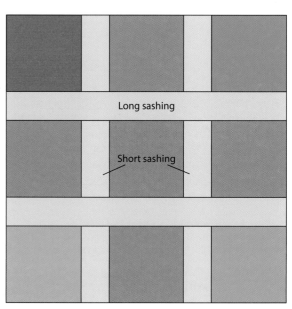

A quilt with sashing only—no sashing squares

One thing to keep in mind is that sashings without sashing squares must be visually continuous from row to row, not mismatched.

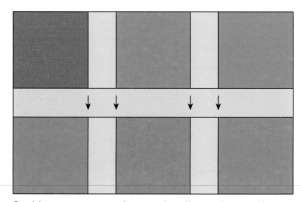

Sashing seams must form a visually continuous line.

To ensure this happens, first sew your blocks and short sashings into rows. Sew a long sashing strip to the first row. Press. Using a pencil and ruler and working from the wrong side, lay the ruler along the seam of the short sashing, extending it past the raw edge of the long sashing. Make a registration mark on the raw edge of the long sashing where the short seam would intersect if it continued across. Repeat for each short sashing seam.

When sewing the next block row to the long sashing, match and pin the short sashing seams of the block row to the registration marks on the edge of the long sashing. This will ensure that the short sashing seams are visually continuous from row to row across the quilt top.

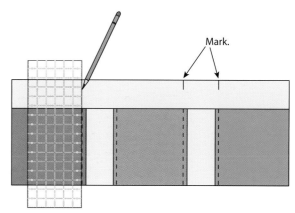

Mark registration lines where the short seam would intersect.

borders

As with big quilts, always measure and cut plain borders to fit the finished width of the quilt top. The process of sewing them to the quilt top is no different than large quilts.

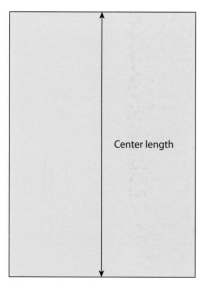

Measure the quilt length through its center to determine the length of side borders.

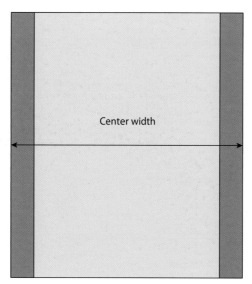

Measure the quilt width through its center to determine the length of top and bottom borders.

If the border has corner squares, measure the center width and length first before adding any borders.

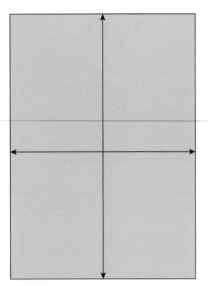

Measure both the center length and width before adding borders. Cut border strips these dimensions.

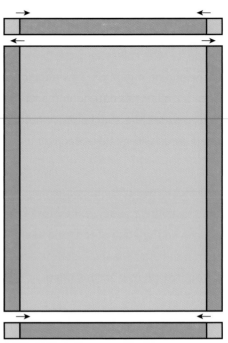

Sew side borders to the quilt. Sew corner squares to top and bottom borders and then sew to quilt top.

If the quilt is a diagonal set, square up the edges to ¼″ from the block points before measuring, cutting, and adding borders.

NOTE

In order to make straight but narrow borders on the Smallest quilts, it's a good practice to cut the border strips wider than needed, sew them into place, and then trim them to finished size plus 1/4″ for the next seam. You may see this reflected in some of the cutting and assembly instructions for the patterns in this book.

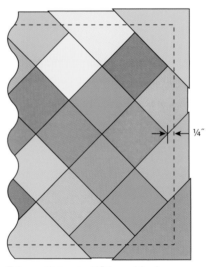

Trim quilt top to ¼″ from block or sashing corners.

backing

As with all quilts, backings should be several inches wider than the quilt top on all sides to allow for quilt draw-in. If pieced, the backing seam may be either horizontal or vertical, depending on the most efficient use of the fabric. For the Small and Smaller quilts, trim it even with the top and batting before binding.

For the Smallest of the quilts, don't trim away the backing completely but rather trim it and roll it to the front to create a rolled binding more in keeping with the scale of the quilt (see Rolled Binding, page 38). Be careful to choose a fabric for the backing that you also wish to have as your binding.

batting

For the Small quilts, you may use your favorite batting, as these quilts are for the most part wallhanging size, although I wouldn't recommend too thick a batting.

For the Smaller quilts, use a thinner batting and preferably cotton so that when washed, it pulls in enough to look like a quilt and not a place mat! The thinner batting will also allow the quilt to drape like a quilt and not be stiff.

For the Smallest quilts, a little more adjustment is necessary. I prefer a very thin wool or cotton batting. To make them thin enough, I peel the batting in half. Not all battings will peel well. My favorite batting is Hobbs Tuscany Collection 100% Wool Batting, which peels beautifully. It makes for a half-density batting that has loft, and it hand or machine quilts like a dream. A craft-size bag will provide you with batts for many miniature quilt.

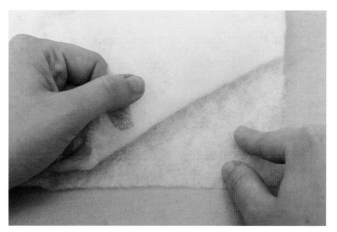

Peel a wool batting in half.

Another favorite is Mountain Mist Blue Ribbon All Cotton Batting. It peels better than most cotton batts although not as nicely as the wool. But it makes for a very thin batt for the tiniest of quilts.

Batts that are glued, needle-punched, or have a mesh scrim will not peel. Play with remnants of other types of cotton batts you have to see what might work.

quilting

The quilting on your quilt must be appropriate to the size of the quilt. Machine or hand quilt the Small quilts as you would normally treat any wallhanging size project. There are no changes in threads, needles, or styles on this larger category of small quilts.

When you get to the Smaller and Smallest quilts, the size of the areas available in which to quilt drops dramatically. Still, there are plenty of ways to quilt these little treasures.

As you can see from the samples in the book, you can both hand and machine quilt the littlest of quilts successfully. You can also mix hand and machine quilting together in one quilt.

Here are a few things to keep in mind when working with the Smaller and Smallest quilts:

- Try not to over-quilt open areas of the quilt with little to no quilting in other parts unless you are trying to create the look of trapunto or raise a design element. The unintended disparity in quilt density can be quite noticeable on small quilts.

- Use lighter-weight threads more appropriate to the size of the quilt. Stick with 50-weight thread but feel free to use the same variety of colors you would on a larger quilt. Be creative, always keeping the scale of the quilt in mind.

- For heavily pieced areas, quilt-in-the-ditch or use outline quilting (⅛″ from the seams). Traditional overall designs such as crosshatching, echo quilting, or Baptist fans, will work well.

- There are many beautiful machine-quilting designs available that are appropriate to the scale of smaller quilts.

- If you're hand quilting, use smaller components of big stencils as designs for your mini masterpieces. A little heart or the small center of a big flower may be just the right size for a small area. Look at your existing stencils with an eye for their smaller components. Additionally, most stencil companies sell quilting stencils designed for miniature borders and blocks that include feathers, cables, and other beautiful designs.

- Make your own tiny free-form stencils. Draw or trace a star, leaf, teardrop, or heart and make it into a simple plastic stencil of your own. Use rulers to mark lines on the top and scallop makers or other tools such as French curves to mark vines. Draw small leaves among the vines. Be creative!

- Use 100% removable chalk or other markings for your quilt designs. *Test first.* Visible lines at this scale are very distracting.

- The half-density batting allows you to make smaller hand-quilting stitches. Use the finest quilting betweens you can manage to enable small stitches.

- Baste your little quilt well if you're planning to hand quilt. The Smallest quilts are too small to hoop. I don't know if basting glue can endure hoopless handling, so I prefer to hand thread baste, which doesn't take long. Tape the backing to a hard surface, with the batting on top, followed by the quilt top marked with the quilting design. Pin baste the layers and follow up with a 1"–2" hand-basted thread grid. Work from the center out so any fullness is moved out to the edges. Finish with a line of basting on the outside edges of the quilt. Remove the tape and you're ready to hand quilt.

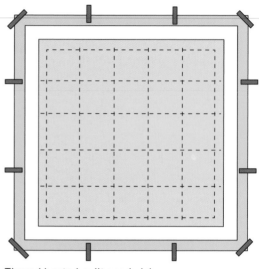

Thread basted quilt sandwich

binding

Wow! It's done and you're ready to bind your small masterpiece.

Double-Fold Binding

For the Small quilts and the larger Smaller quilts, you can bind with a standard double-fold binding. Use your favorite method, but cut the strips no more than 1¾" wide, or, better yet, cut them 1⅝" wide. You want a finished binding no wider than ¼".

Single-Fold Binding

For the Smallest quilts and in special cases for the Smaller quilts, for proper scale, the binding should be ³⁄₁₆" wide, which is narrower than the ¼" standard on larger quilts. A double-fold binding is also too thick for the scale of the quilt. A narrow single-fold binding is often the better choice for an applied binding.

First, trim the batting and backing even with the quilt top and square up the corners. Then follow these steps to make and apply a single-fold binding.

1 Cut a single fold binding six times wider than the desired finished width of the binding. So to make a ³⁄₁₆"-wide binding, cut strips 1⅛ wide.

If you prefer to use a full ¼" binding, cut the strips 1¼" wide.

2 Add the lengths of the four sides of the quilt. Add 6"–8" to this. Divide by the width of your fabric to determine the number of binding strips you need. Sew them together end to end with diagonal seams. Press seams to one side.

Sew binding strips together with diagonal seams. Trim excess away ¼" from seam.

3 Beginning in the middle of one side, place one raw binding edge on the trimmed edge of the quilt top leaving an unsewn 3″–4″ starting tail. Using a ³⁄₁₆″ seam, sew up to ³⁄₁₆″ from the first corner. Back-stitch and stop.

Leave an ending tail and start sewing from the middle of one side.

4 Flip the binding straight up so it runs parallel to the next side.

Flip the tail straight up so it runs parallel to the next side.

5 Fold the binding back down onto the next side, pinning the pleat formed at the corner in place. Start stitching at the edge, continuing on to the next corner. Repeat the process for all four corners.

Flip the tail straight down, aligning it with the edge of the next side.

6 After turning the last corner, stitch a short distance on the final side, backstitch, and remove the quilt from the machine to prepare joining the binding tails. Cut the ending and beginning tails so they overlap by at least 2″. Lay the ending tail under the starting tail, aligning both strips with the edge of the quilt. Pin all the layers smooth as they will be when stitched down.

7 Make a mark 1⅛″ in from the end of the starting tail. Cut the ending tail to this length.

Trim and overlap the ending tail with the starting tail. Mark starting tail.

8 Unpin the tails and place them right sides together at a 45° angle. Stitch across the diagonal.

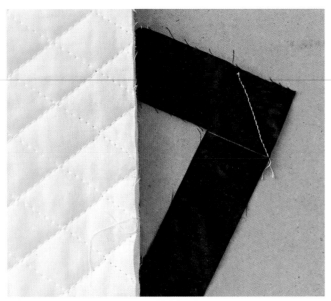

Sew the tails together with a diagonal seam.

9 Check to make sure the strips aren't twisted, then trim the excess corner to ¼″ from the seam and press to one side. Lay the binding back in place and finish the last bit of stitching.

Finish the rest of the binding seam.

10 Roll the binding to the back and fold it in half. Slipstitch the fold to the back of the quilt as you would normally, being sure to miter and stitch the corners as well.

rolled binding

While a single-fold binding will work on the Smallest quilts when you want to use a diagonal stripe or pieced binding, in most cases, the best binding for the Smallest quilts is rolled binding. It's made by rolling the backing around to the front to create a binding.

When using a rolled binding, choose a backing that is also what you want for the binding. Be very careful not to quilt to within a ¼″ of the raw edge of the quilt. That area must be left unstitched in order to trim the batting.

A rolled binding is very simple to make.

1 Fold and pin the backing completely out of the way of the batting and quilt top. Trim the batting even with the quilt top, being very careful not to snip the backing in the process.

NOTE
If you accidentally snip your backing, you'll have to switch gears and use a single-fold binding (see Single-Fold Binding, page 36).

2 Lay the backing back out flat and trim it to ½″ from the quilt top.

Trim the batting even with the quilt top. Then trim the backing ½″ wider.

3 Working with one side at a time, fold the backing in half to meet the edge of the quilt top.

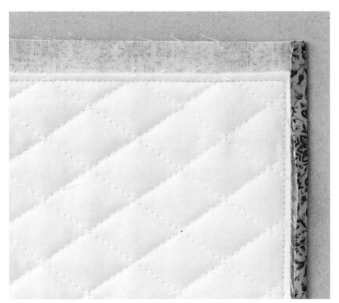

Fold backing in half.

4 Roll the folded backing to the front of the quilt. Secure it with pins or binding clips and begin slip-stitching it to the front of the quilt with a fine, closely matching thread and tiny stitches.

Roll backing fold to the front of the quilt top and slipstitch it in place.

5 Before getting to the corner, evenly finger-press the fold completely past the corner.

6 Turn over the fold to make a triangle. Secure with a pin or clip. Fold the backing on the next side in half and roll it to the front. The corner turn in the fold should form a pleat at the corner. Secure it with a pin or binding clip.

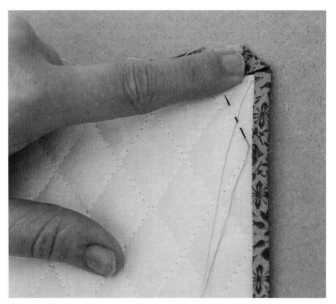

Fold and roll corner to make a diagonal pleat.

7 Continue slipstitching to the corner. Slipstitch the pleat in place. Roll and fold the backing into place on the remaining sides.

And ... drum roll ... your quilt is done! Don't forget to put a little label on it so future generations will be just as impressed as your friends are now!

THE QUILTS

Here's where the fun begins! There are twelve patterns in this book on which to practice your miniature quilt-making skills, and they are categorized into three skill levels:

 The **Testing the Waters** quilts are made using simple techniques like basic strip piecing. They're a good stepping-stone into working with smaller pieces.

 The **Easing In** quilts feature half-square triangle units (HST units) and there is a bit more complexity to the designs.

 Finally, the **Diving In** quilts are a bit more intricate in their piecing and require a bit more patience and accuracy.

Within each of the twelve patterns, there's the option to make the quilt in two or three block sizes. Eight patterns offer three block sizes while four patterns have only two. All patterns present a different sample for each size, allowing you to see multiple ways to color the quilt. With three sizes available, you can master skills and work your way down to the world of the teeny-tiny!

Because of the different sizes, there are charts for both fabric requirements and cutting instructions. Find the chart section for the size quilt you are making and cut the pieces listed for each fabric.

Since there are multiple color samples for each pattern, the different prints are generically referred to as fabric A, B, C, and so on, to avoid referring to specific colors. I highly recommend that you make a swatch card reflecting your individual color choices for each fabric listed in the chart. Using a piece of paper or 3″ × 5″ cards, record your fabric selections for each fabric listed.

If the pattern requires multiple prints for one or more "fabrics," use one card for each fabric and glue swatches of all your choices or a descriptor that covers the range of your choices on that one card. It can be easy to get confused if you don't make some sort of guide or swatch cards to help you keep track of your prints.

Fabric requirements can be small or odd-size in some of these quilts. Please note they are the *minimum* you need. So, if a pattern lists a 7″ × 12″ piece of fabric, it isn't necessary to cut a fat eighth or fat quarter into that size since a fat eighth or quarter is more than big enough. But alternately, this is very helpful information if you are choosing fabrics from odd sizes of scraps in your stash. If you have a 9″ × 14″ chunk of fabric in your stash that you'd like to use, you'll know you have enough. If it's 6″ × 10″, you know it won't work because it's smaller than the 7″ × 12″ minimum needed.

The quilt sizes are categorized as follows:

Small quilts are the samples with the biggest finished-size blocks, generally ranging between 4″ and 6″.

Smaller quilts have blocks in the 3″ to 4″ range with some exceptions.

Smallest quilts have blocks that finish smaller than 3″.

Because most of the Small quilts are larger wallhanging or table-topper size, they are bound with normal double-fold binding. It's up to you whether you use a double-fold or single-fold binding on the Small quilts. Please note that all binding cutting and yardages are based on a double-fold binding, meaning that if you choose a single-fold binding, you'll have leftover yardage. The Smallest quilts are best finished and bound using the backing as a rolled binding (see Rolled Binding, page 38).

FRACTURED

Simple to make in any color and any size, this quilt looks great without any borders.

 Skill level: Testing the Waters

Small *Fractured*, 33½″ × 33½″, pieced by Cynthia Ann Burgess, machine quilted by Denise Mariano, 2017

Smaller *Fractured*, 24½″ × 24½″, pieced and machine quilted by Katharine Brigham, 2016

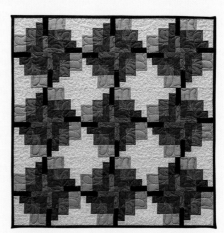

Smallest *Fractured*, 15½″ × 15½″, designed and pieced by Donna Lynn Thomas, machine quilted by Theresa Ward, 2017

MATERIALS

Quilt size	Very dark	Dark	Medium	Light	Accent	Background	Backing	Binding
SMALL	⅓ yard	⅓ yard	½ yard	⅜ yard	¼ yard	⅝ yard	1⅛ yards	¼ yard
SMALLER	¼ yard	¼ yard	⅜ yard	¼ yard	¼ yard	⅜ yard	⅞ yard	¼ yard
SMALLEST	8″ × 11″	8″ × 12″	14″ × 15″	11″ × 12″	10″ × 14″	12″ × 24″	½ yard	—

select fabrics

Choose one color family for your quilt and then choose a very dark, a dark, a medium, and a light print or solid from that chosen color. Choose a second color family for the accent.

CUTTING

Very dark	Dark	Medium	Light	Accent	Background	Backing and batting	Binding
SMALL Finished quilt: 33½″ × 33½″ • Finished block: 5½″ × 5½″							
4 strips 3¼″ × 15″ for strip set 1	4 strips 3¼″ × 18″ for strip set 2	4 strips 3¼″ × 15″ for strip set 1 4 strips 3¼″ × 20″ for strip set 3	6 strips 3¼″ × 15″ for strip set 4	4 strips 2″ × 18″ for strip set 2 4 strips 1¼″ × 20″ for strip set 3	4 strips 1¾″ × 18″ for strip set 2 4 strips 2½″ × 20″ for strip set 3 6 strips 3¼″ × 15″ for strip set 4	39″ × 39″ square	4 strips 1¾″ × 40″
SMALLER Finished quilt: 24½″ × 24½″ • Finished block: 4″ × 4″							
4 strips 2½″ × 12″ for strip set 1	4 strips 2½″ × 14″ for strip set 2	4 strips 2½″ × 12″ for strip set 1 4 strips 2½″ × 17″ for strip set 3	6 strips 2½″ × 13″ for strip set 4	4 strips 1⅞″ × 14″ for strip set 2 4 strips 1⅛″ × 17″ for strip set 3	4 strips 1⅛″ × 14″ for strip set 2 4 strips 1⅞″ × 17″ for strip set 3 6 strips 2½″ × 13″ for strip set 4	29″ × 29″ square	3 strips 1¾″ × 40″
SMALLEST Finished quilt: 15½″ × 15½″ • Finished block: 2½″ × 2½″							
4 strips 1¾″ × 10″ for strip set 1	4 strips 1¾″ × 11″ for strip set 2	4 strips 1¾″ × 10″ for strip set 1 4 strips 1¾″ × 13″ for strip set 3	6 strips 1¾″ × 10″ for strip set 4	4 strips 1⅜″ × 11″ for strip set 2 4 strips ⅞″ × 13″ for strip set 3	4 strips ⅞″ × 11″ for strip set 2 4 strips 1⅜″ × 13″ for strip set 3 6 strips 1¾″ × 10″ for strip set 4	18″ × 18″ square	—

make the block

Press all the seams in the direction of the arrows indicated in the drawings. For the Smallest version, trim the seams to ⅛″ after sewing.

1 Make 4 each of strip sets 1, 2, and 3. Make 6 of strip set 4. Press all the seams to the darkest print. Cut a total of 36 segments from each group of strip sets. Refer to the Segment Cutting chart for the width to cut segments from each of the strip sets for your quilt. *Figs. A–D*

SEGMENT CUTTING

Quilt size	Strip set 1	Strip set 2	Strip set 3	Strip set 4
	Cut 36 segments from each strip set.			
SMALL	1½″ wide	1¾″ wide	2″ wide	2¼″ wide
SMALLER	1⅛″ wide	1⅜″ wide	1⅝″ wide	1⅞″ wide
SMALLEST	⅞″ wide	1″ wide	1¼″ wide	1⅜″ wide

2 Sew one of each segment together to make a block. Make 36. *Fig. E*

A. Strip set 1: Make 4. Cut 36 segments.

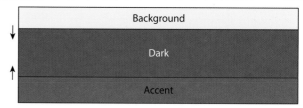

B. Strip set 2: Make 4. Cut 36 segments.

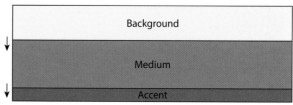

C. Strip set 3: Make 4. Cut 36 segments.

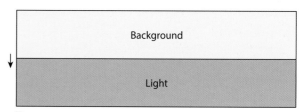

D. Strip set 4: Make 6. Cut 36 segments.

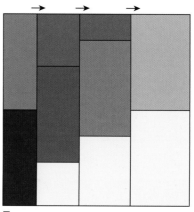

E

make the quilt top

1 Sew the blocks into rows as shown. *Fig. A*

2 Sew the rows together. Press so the final center seam spins clockwise. *Fig. B*

3 Sew the 4-block units into 3 rows of 3 units each. Press block seams in alternate directions from row to row. *Fig. C*

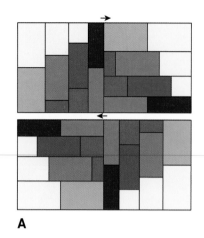

A

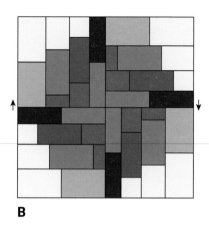

B

finish the quilt top

1 Layer and baste the quilt.

2 Quilt as desired.

3 Bind the quilt. Bind the Small and Smaller versions with binding strips. For the Smallest version, use the backing to create a rolled binding (see Rolled Binding, page 38).

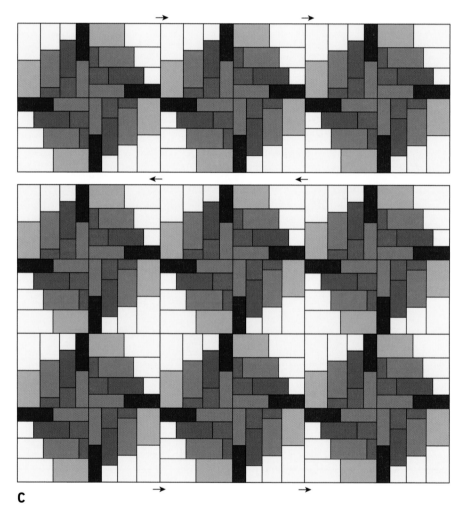

C

PRIMARY SQUARES

This is a fun and easy block that allows you to use a lot of color for a lively effect. After my blocks were done, I stumbled across the tiny Laurel Burch print in my stash, which was perfect for the border.

Skill level:
Testing the
Waters

Small *Primary Squares*, 28¼″ × 28¼″, pieced by Barbara Gerdes Fife, machine quilted by Lee Robertson, 2016

Smaller *Primary Squares*, 19″ × 19″, pieced and hand quilted by Linda Birch Mooney, 2017

Smallest *Primary Squares*, 10″ × 10″, designed and pieced by Donna Lynn Thomas, machine quilted by Theresa Ward, 2017

MATERIALS

Quilt size	Print A: 8 prints	Print B: 8 prints	Print C: 8 prints	Print D: Outer border and binding	Print E: Inner border	Backing
SMALL	5″ × 20″ piece of each	6″ × 7″ piece of each	4″ × 20″ piece of each	⅜ yard	½ yard	1 yard
SMALLER	6″ × 10″ piece of each	5″ × 5″ piece of each	4″ × 10″ piece of each	16″ × 20″ piece	10″ × 20″ piece	¾ yard
SMALLEST	3″ × 10″ piece of each	4″ × 4″ piece of each	3″ × 8″ piece of each	6″ × 10″ piece of each	8″ × 10″ piece	13″ × 13″ square

select fabrics

Make these charming blocks 2 at a time using 8 sets of prints for a total of 16 blocks. Choose a multicolor print for the border. Choose 2 coordinating prints and a background print for each pair of blocks, using the multicolor print as a guide for color choices.

Print A: Color band around the block (turquoise in diagrams)

Print B: Forms the cross bars through the middle (pink in diagrams)

Print C: Light band in each block (cream in diagrams)

Print D: Multicolor print for the outer border

Print E: Inner border

CUTTING

Print A: From each of 8 prints	Print B: From *each* of 8 prints	Print C: From *each* of 8 background prints	Print D: Multicolor print	Print E: Inner border	Backing and batting
SMALL *Finished quilt: 28¼″ × 28¼″* • *Finished block: 5¼″ × 5¼″*					
1 strip 1¼″ × 11″ for strip set 8 rectangles 1¼″ × 2″ 8 rectangles 1¼″ × 2¾″	8 rectangles 1¼″ × 2¾″	1 strip 1¼″ × 11″ for strip set 8 rectangles 1¼″ × 2″ 2 squares 1¼″ × 1¼″	4 strips 1⅝″ × 40″ for outer border 3 strips 1¾″ × 40″ for binding	4 strips 2¾″ × 40″	34″ × 34″ square
SMALLER *Finished quilt: 19″ × 19″* • *Finished block: 3½″ × 3½″*					
1 strip 1″ × 9″ for strip set 8 rectangles 1″ × 1½″ 8 rectangles 1″ × 2″	8 rectangles 1″ × 2″	1 strip 1″ × 9″ for strip set 8 rectangles 1″ × 1½″ 2 squares 1″ × 1″	4 strips 1¼″ × 20″ for outer border 5 strips 1¾″ × 20″ for binding	4 strips 2″ × 20″	24″ × 24″ square
SMALLEST *Finished quilt: 10″ × 10″* • *Finished block: 1¾″ × 1¾″*					
1 strip ¾″ × 7″ for strip set 8 rectangles ¾″ × 1″ 8 rectangles ¾″ × 1¼″	8 rectangles ¾″ × 1¼″	1 strip ¾″ × 7″ for strip set 8 rectangles ¾″ × 1″ 2 squares ¾ ″ × ¾″	4 strips 1″ × 10″ for outer border	4 strips 1¼″ × 10″	14″ × 14″ square

make a pair of blocks

Group your pieces into 8 sets consisting of the pieces from 1 print A, 1 print B, and one background print. Each set will yield 2 blocks. Press all the seams in the direction of the arrows indicated in the drawings. For the Smallest version, trim the seams to ⅛″ after sewing.

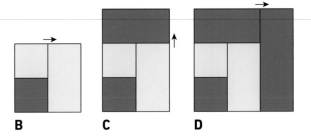

A

1 Sew the print A and print C strips together to make 1 strip set. (*Fig. A*) Cut 8 segments from the strip set. Refer to this list for the segment width:

Small quilt: Cut segments 1¼″ wide.

Smaller quilt: Cut segments 1″ wide.

Smallest quilt: Cut segments ¾″ wide.

2 Sew each segment to a print C rectangle. Make 8. *Fig. B*

3 Using the 2 different-size print A rectangles and the units from Step 2, make 8 corner units. *Figs. C & D*

4 Sew 4 print B rectangles, 4 corner units, and 1 print C square together into rows. *Fig. E*

5 Sew rows together to make a block. Make 2 blocks. *Fig. F*

6 Repeat Steps 1–5 with each set of prints to make a total of 16 blocks.

B   **C**   **D**

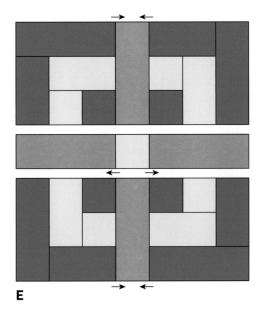

E

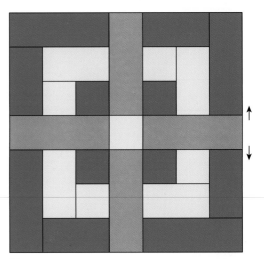

F

make the quilt top

1 Arrange the assorted blocks into 4 rows of 4 blocks each. Balance the blocks so like colors are dispersed and not clustered together. Rotate block position by one-quarter turn as needed so seams nest where the blocks meet.

2 Join the blocks into rows, pressing seams in alternate directions from row to row. Join the rows to complete the quilt center.

3 Referring to Sewing Borders (page 33), measure, cut, and sew the inner border to the top followed by the outer border.

finish the quilt top

1 Layer and baste the quilt.

2 Quilt as desired.

3 Bind the quilt. Bind the Small and Smaller versions with single- or double-fold binding strips. For the Smallest version, use the backing to create a rolled binding (see Rolled Binding, page 38).

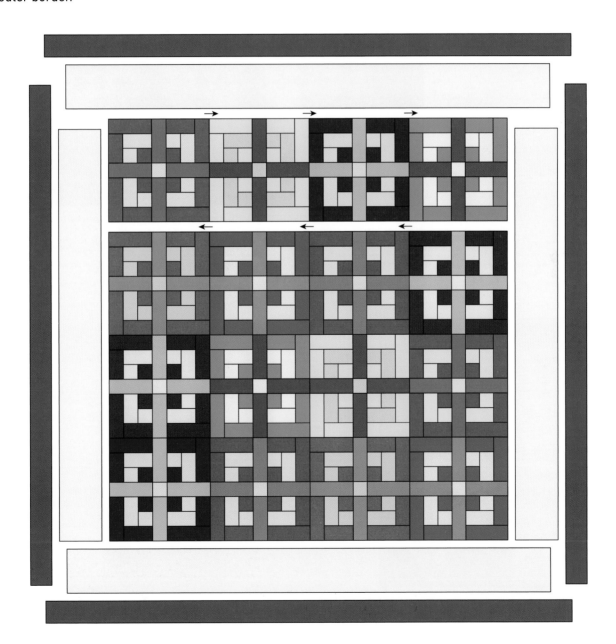

CHARMED, I'M SURE

After finding a charm pack of solids and a fat quarter of cream while on a quilt cruise, I set out to design and sew a little quilt and this was the result. The smallest blocks really need only half of a charm square for each block!

 Skill level: Testing the Waters

Small *Charmed, I'm Sure*, 30½″ × 30½″, with a modified outer border, pieced by Barbara Gerdes Fife, machine quilted by Lee Robertson, 2016

Smaller *Charmed, I'm Sure*, 18″ × 18″, with a modified inner border and omitted the outer border, pieced and hand quilted by Linda Birch Mooney, 2017

Smallest *Charmed, I'm Sure*, 11½″ × 11½″, pieced, hand and machine quilted by Donna Lynn Thomas, 2015

MATERIALS

Quilt size	Fabric A: 13 assorted prints	Fabric B: Background	Fabric C: Side-setting triangles and outer border	Fabric D: Inner border	Backing and binding
SMALL	5″ × 9″ piece each	½ yard	⅞ yard	½ yard	1⅛ yard
SMALLER	4″ × 8″ piece each	⅜ yard	⅝ yard	⅓ yard	⅞ yard
SMALLEST	5″ × 5″ square each	10″ × 20″ piece	13″ × 13″ square	1″ × 10″ each piece of 4 solids	14″ × 14″ square

select fabrics

Each of the 13 blocks is made from a different fabric and one background fabric. Choose 13 different fabrics for the blocks (fabric A). Choose 1 background fabric to use in all the blocks (fabric B). Then choose a dark fabric for the side-setting triangles and outer border (fabric C). If you prefer, you can choose 2 fabrics—one for the side-setting triangles and one for the border. Divide the yardage needed for fabric C if you decide to do this.

Fabric A: 13 different fabrics for the blocks (dark gray in diagrams)

Fabric B: Background fabric used in all the blocks (light gray in diagrams)

Fabric C: Side-setting triangles and outer border (black in diagram)

Fabric D: Inner border. The Smallest version has 4 different border fabrics for the inner border. The Small and Smaller quilts have only one.

CUTTING

Fabric A: 13 assorted fabrics	Fabric B: Background	Fabric C: Side-setting triangles and outer border	Fabric D: Inner border and binding	Backing and batting
SMALL *Finished quilt: 31½″ × 31½″ • Finished block: 5″ × 5″*				
2 strips 1½″ × 7″ 1 square 1½″ × 1½″	9 strips 1½″ × 40″; subcut 26 strips 1½″ × 7″ 52 rectangles 1½″ × 2½″	2 squares 8⅜″ × 8⅜″ ⊠ 2 squares 4½″ × 4½″ ☐ 4 strips 4½″ × 40″ for outer border	4 strips 1⅜″ × 40″ for inner border 4 strips 1¾″ × 40″ for binding	37″ × 37″ square
SMALLER *Finished quilt: 24⅛″ × 24⅛″ • Finished block: 3¾″ × 3¾″*				
2 strips 1¼″ × 6″ 1 square 1¼″ × 1¼″	7 strips 1¼″ × 40″; subcut 26 strips 1¼″ × 6″ 52 rectangles 1¼″ × 2″	2 squares 6⅝″ × 6⅝″ ⊠ 2 squares 3⅝″ × 3⅝″ ☐ 3 strips 3¾″ × 40″ for outer border	4 strips 1⅛″ × 18″ for inner border 3 strips 1¾″ × 40″ for binding	29″ × 29″ square
SMALLEST *Finished quilt: 11½″ × 11½″ • Finished block: 1⅞″ × 1⅞″*				
2 strips ⅞″ × 5″ 1 square ⅞″ × ⅞″	10 strips ⅞″ × 20″; subcut 26 strips ⅞″ × 5″ 52 rectangles ⅞″ × 1¼″	2 squares 4¼″ × 4¼″ ⊠ 2 squares 2¼″ × 2¼″ ☐ 4 strips 1¾″ × 13″ for outer border	**From each of 4 inner border solids:** 1 strip 1″ × 10″ for inner border	14″ × 14″ square

Key:
☐ *= Cut the squares once diagonally to make half-square triangles.*
⊠ *= Cut the squares twice diagonally to make quarter-square triangles.*

make a block

Group your pieces into 13 sets consisting of the pieces from 1 fabric A and the background fabric. Each set will yield 1 block. Press all the seams in the direction of the arrows indicated in the drawings. For the Smallest version, trim the seams to ⅛˝ after sewing.

1 Sew each of the fabric A strips to a fabric B strip. Make 2 strip sets. (*Fig. A*) Cut a total of 8 segments from the 2 strip sets. Refer to this list for the segment width:

Small quilt: Cut 8 segments 1½˝ wide.

Smaller quilt: Cut 8 segments 1¼˝ wide.

Smallest quilt: Cut 8 segments ⅞˝ wide.

2 Sew 2 segments together to make a four-patch unit. Be careful to lay them out and sew them consistently as shown. Make 4. Press seams in a counterclockwise direction. *Fig. B*

3 Arrange the four-patch units, 4 cream rectangles, and the fabric A square as shown. Sew the pieces into rows. *Fig. C*

4 Join the rows together to complete a block. *Fig. D*

5 Repeat Steps 1–4 to make a total of 13 blocks, each with a different fabric A.

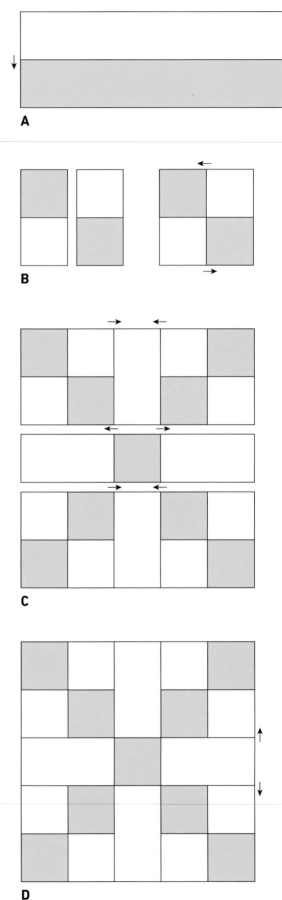

A

B

C

D

make the quilt top

1 Arrange the blocks into a pleasing diagonal quilt set, balancing warm and cool colors across the quilt top. Refer to the quilt photo (page 52) for assistance. Add the fabric C quarter-square triangles to the ends of the rows. Rotate the blocks one-quarter turn as needed so the seams joining the blocks together will nest. *Fig. A*

2 Sew the blocks into rows and then join the rows together, pressing seams in alternate direction from row to row. Sew the 4 corner half-square triangles on last. Trim the quilt top to ¼″ from the block corners.

3 Measure across the quilt top, as shown in Sewing Borders (page 33). However, each border will be cut this length plus the finished width of the border. If your blocks were sewn with a correct ¼″ seam, then the borders will be cut these lengths:

Small quilt: 22⅝″

Smaller quilt: 17⅛″

Smallest quilt: 9⅛″

4 Sew the first inner border strip to the quilt top leaving about 2″ unsewn ay the end. Sew the remaining borders to the sides of the quilt in the order indicated. Once the fourth border strip is in place, go back and finish sewing the last 2″ of the first border. Press the seams away from the quilt center. For the Smallest quilt only, carefully trim all 4 sides of the oversized border to ½″ wide, measuring from the seam. *Fig. B*

A

B. Numbered arrows indicate the order and direction to sew.

5 Referring to Sewing Borders (page 33), measure, cut, and sew the outer border strips to the quilt sides first then to the top and bottom. Press the seams away from the center of the quilt. *Fig. C*

C

finish the quilt top

1 Layer and baste the quilt.

2 Quilt as desired.

3 Bind the quilt. Bind the Small and Smaller versions with single- or double-fold binding strips. For the Smallest version, use the backing to create a rolled binding (see Rolled Binding, page 38).

PAT'S WARP AND WEFT

I designed this little quilt in memory of my beloved mother-in-law, Pat Thomas, a spinner and weaver. My red, black, and gray version reminds me of a woven tartan plaid, while Kari Hoyes changed up her quilt a bit by using a variety of dark prints instead of just one.

 Skill level: Testing the Waters

Small *Pat's Warp and Weft*, 30½″ × 42½″, pieced and machine quilted by Kari Hoyes, 2017

Smallest *Pat's Warp and Weft*, 15½″ × 21½″, designed and pieced by Donna Lynn Thomas, machine quilted by Denise Mariano, 2017

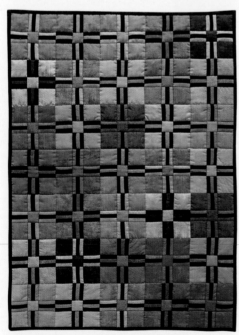

Smaller *Pat's Warp and Weft*, 23⅝″ × 32⅞″, pieced and machine quilted by Kelly Ashton, 2017

MATERIALS

Quilt size	Print A: 1 dark print (or 9 different prints)	Print B: 9 medium prints	Print C: 9 light prints	Backing	Binding
SMALL	⅞ yard or ⅛ yard each	¼ yard each	¼ yard each	1⅓ yards	¼ yard
SMALLER	⅜ yard or ⅛ yard each	7″ × 20″ piece each	8″ × 20″ piece each	⅞ yard	¼ yard
SMALLEST	15″ × 22″ piece or 6″ × 8″ piece each	7″ × 7″ square each	7″ × 8″ piece each	½ yard	—

select fabrics

The block is colored in two ways to create a checker-board feel. Make 9 pairs of block 1 and 9 pairs of block 2. Depending on how you arrange your blocks you will have 1 leftover block 1 or block 2.

Choose 9 sets of coordinated medium and light print combinations. Use 1 set of medium and light prints to make 2 of block 1 and 2 of block 2. Notice how the 3 prints are arranged differently in the 2 blocks (at right).

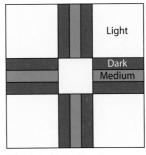

Block 1: Make 9 pairs.

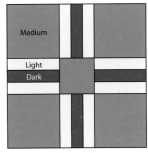

Block 2: Make 9 pairs.

CUTTING

Print A: From dark print or from each of 9 medium prints	Print B: From each of 9 medium prints	Print C: From each of 9 light prints	Backing and batting	Binding
SMALL Finished quilt: 30½″ × 42½″ • Finished block: 6″ × 6″				
Block 1: 18 strips 1″ × 24″ for strip sets	**Block 1:** 1 strip 1″ × 24″ for strip set	**Block 1:** 8 squares 2¾″ × 2¾″ 2 squares 2″ × 2″	36″ × 48″	4 strips 1¾″ × 40″
Block 2: 9 strips 1″ × 24″ for strip sets	**Block 2:** 8 squares 2¾″ × 2¾″ 2 squares 2″ × 2″	**Block 2:** 2 strips 1″ × 24″ for strip set		
SMALLER Finished quilt: 23⅝″ × 32⅞″ • Finished block: 4⅝″ × 4⅝″				
Block 1: 18 strips ⅞″ × 20″ for strip sets	**Block 1:** 1 strip ⅞″ × 20″ for strip set	**Block 1:** 8 squares 2¼″ × 2¼″ 2 squares 1⅝″ × 1⅝″	29″ × 38″	3 strips 1¾″ × 40″
Block 2: 9 strips ⅞″ × 20″ for strip sets	**Block 2:** 8 squares 2¼″ × 2¼″ 2 squares 1⅝″ × 1⅝″	**Block 2:** 2 strips ⅞″ × 20″ for strip set		
SMALLEST Finished quilt: 15½″ × 21½″ • Finished block: 3″ × 3″				
Block 1: 36 strips ¾″ × 7″ for strip sets	**Block 1:** 2 strips ¾″ × 7″ for strip set	**Block 1:** 8 squares 1⅝″ × 1⅝″ 2 squares 1¼″ × 1¼″	18″ × 24″	—
Block 2: 18 strips ¾″ × 7″ for strip sets	**Block 2:** 8 squares 1⅝″ × 1⅝″ 2 squares 1¼″ × 1¼″	**Block 2:** 4 strips ¾″ × 7″ for strip set		

make a pair of block 1

Use the 9 sets consisting of the pieces for a pair of block 1. Each set will yield 2 blocks. Press all the seams in the direction of the arrows indicated in the drawings. For the Smallest version, trim the seams to ⅛″ after sewing.

1 Sew 2 print A dark strips and 1 print B medium strip together to make 1 strip set each for the Small and Smaller quilts and 2 strip sets each for the Smallest quilt. (*Fig. A*) Cut 8 segments from the strip set(s). Refer to this list for the segment width:

Small quilt: Cut 8 segments 2¾″ wide.

Smaller quilt: Cut 8 segments 2¼″ wide.

Smallest quilt: Cut 8 segments 1⅝″ wide.

2 Arrange 4 segments, 1 print C light small center square, and 4 print C large squares as shown. Sew them into rows. *Fig. B*

3 Join the rows together to complete a block. Make 2. *Fig. C*

4 Repeat Steps 1–3 using the remaining block 1 sets of cut pieces. Make 9 pairs for a total of 18 blocks.

A

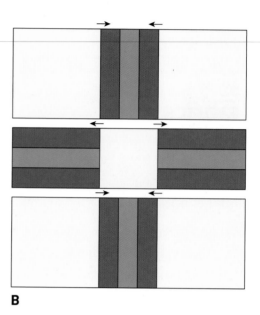

B

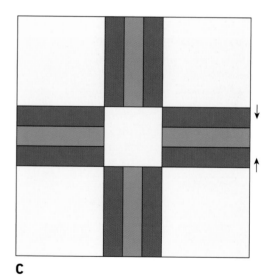

C

make a pair of block 2

Follow these instructions, using the pieces for block 2. Press the seams in the direction indicated by the arrows.

A

1 Sew 1 print A dark strip and 2 print C light strips together to make 1 strip set each for the Small and Smaller quilts and 2 strip sets each for the Smallest quilt. (*Fig. A*) Cut 8 segments from the strip set(s). Refer to this list for the segment width:

Small quilt: Cut 8 segments 2¾″ wide.

Smaller quilt: Cut 8 segments 2¼″ wide.

Smallest quilt: Cut 8 segments 1⅝″ wide.

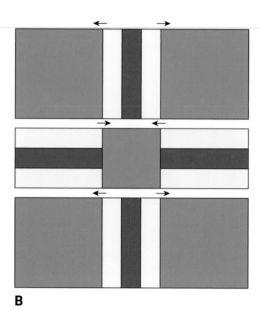

2 Arrange 4 segments, a print B small center square, and 4 large print B squares as shown. Sew them into rows. *Fig. B*

3 Join the rows together to complete a block. Make 2. *Fig. C*

B

4 Repeat Steps 1–3 using the remaining block 2 sets of cut pieces. Make 9 pairs for a total of 18 blocks.

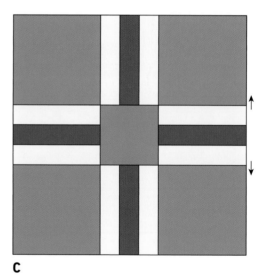

C

make the quilt top

1 Arrange the assorted blocks into 7 rows of 5 blocks each. Alternate block 1 and block 2 and balance the colors so they are dispersed and not clustered together. You'll have 1 leftover block.

2 Join the blocks into rows, pressing seams in alternate directions from row to row. Join the rows to complete the quilt center.

finish the quilt top

1 Layer and baste the quilt.

2 Quilt as desired.

3 Bind the quilt. Bind the Small and Smaller versions with single- or double-fold binding strips. For the Smallest version, use the backing to create a rolled binding (see Rolled Binding, page 38).

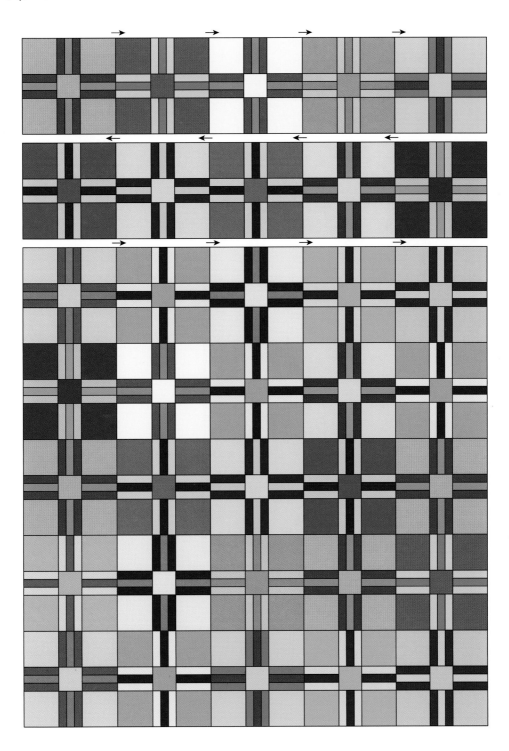

PARADE

I made a full-size version of this quilt years ago and have been itching to make it small. The little one brightens my day just as much as the big one.

Skill level: Easing In

Smaller *Parade*, 24½″ × 32½″, pieced and hand quilted by Linda Birch Mooney, 2017

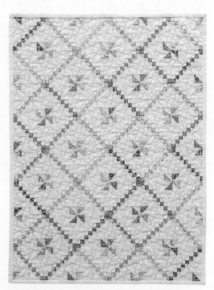

Smallest *Parade*, 12½″ × 16½″, designed and pieced by Donna Lynn Thomas, machine quilted by Theresa Ward, 2017

MATERIALS

Quilt size	Fabric A: 12 dark prints	Fabric B: Background print	Backing	Binding
SMALLER	5″ × 20″ piece each	1½ yards	⅞ yard	¼ yard
SMALLEST	4″ × 13″ piece each	⅝ yard	15″ × 19″	—

select fabrics

Make 48 blocks in 12 sets of 4 blocks, using a different print with each set of blocks. Use one background print for all the blocks.

CUTTING

Fabric A: From each of 12 dark prints	Fabric B: Background print	Backing and batting	Binding
SMALLER *Finished quilt: 24½″ × 32½″ • Finished block: 4″ × 4″*			
2 strips 1″ × 20″ for strip sets 4 squares 2″ × 2″ ◲ for HST units	12 strips 1″ × 40″; subcut 24 strips 1″ × 20″ for strip sets 3 strips 2″ × 40″; subcut 48 squares 2″ × 2″ ◲ for HST units 18 strips 1½″ × 40″; subcut 288 squares 1½″ × 1½″ and 96 rectangles 1½″ × 2½″ for block piecing	29″ × 37″	3 strips, 1¾″ × 40″
SMALLEST *Finished quilt: 12½″ × 16½″ • Finished block: 2″ × 2″*			
2 strips ¾″ × 13″ for strip sets 4 squares 1½″ × 1½″ ◲ for HST units	8 strips ¾″ × 40″; subcut 24 strips ¾″ × 13″ for strip sets 2 strips 1½″ × 40″; subcut 48 squares 1½″ × 1½″ ◲ for HST units 12 strips 1″ × 40″; subcut 288 squares 1″ × 1″ and 96 rectangles 1″ × 1½″ for block piecing	15″ × 19″	—

Key: ◲ = Cut those squares once diagonally to make half-square triangles.

make a block

Group your pieces into 12 sets consisting of the pieces from one fabric A, and the pieces from the background print. Each set will yield 4 blocks. Press all the seams in the direction of the arrows indicated in the drawings. For the Smallest version, trim the seams to ⅛″ after sewing.

1 Using the 2 dark strips and 2 background strips, make 2 strip sets. (*Fig. A*) Cut a total of 32 segments. Refer to this list for the segment width:

Smaller quilt: Cut 32 segments 1″ wide.

Smallest quilt: Cut 32 segments ¾″ wide.

2 Arrange the segments and sew them into four-patches. Make 16. Pop the center seam so the seams flow in a clockwise direction when looking at the front of the block. *Fig. B*

3 Sew together 2 four-patches and 2 fabric B squares to make a double four-patch. Make 8. *Fig. C*

4 Using the 8 fabric A and 8 fabric B half-square triangles, make 8 half-square triangle units. (*Fig. D*) Trim to these sizes:

Smaller quilt: Trim to 1½″.

Smallest quilt: Trim to 1″.

5 Sew together a half-square triangle unit, a fabric B square, and a fabric B rectangle as shown. Make 8. *Fig. E*

6 Arrange 2 units from Step 3 and 2 units from Step 5 as shown and sew together. *Fig. F*

7 Sew the units together to complete a block. Make 4. Pop the center seam joining the half-blocks together. If done correctly, the seams on the perimeter of the block should all flow in a clockwise direction when looking at the front of the block. *Fig. G*

8 Repeat Steps 1–7 with each dark print to make a total of 48 blocks.

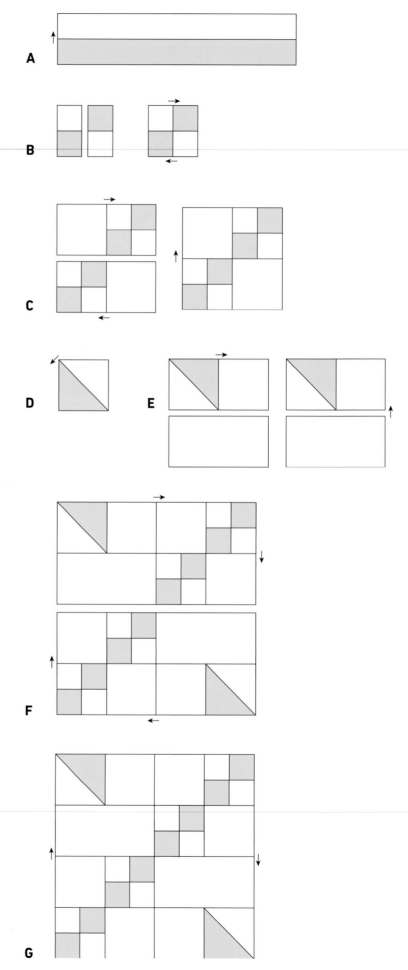

make the quilt top

Referring to the quilt diagram, arrange the blocks into 8 rows of 6 blocks each, turning them so pinwheels form at the corners where the blocks meet. Sew the blocks into row, nesting seams as they meet. Press the seams in opposite directions from row to row. Join the rows together to complete the quilt top.

finish the quilt top

1 Layer and baste the quilt.

2 Quilt as desired.

3 Bind the quilt. Bind the Smaller version with single- or double-fold binding strips. For the Smallest version, use the backing to create a rolled binding (see Rolled Binding, page 38).

STAR CROSSED

No matter what theme you choose for your quilt, each Sawtooth Star print will shine in its own block surrounded by chains of color.

 Skill level:
Easing In

Small *Star Crossed*, 24½″ × 32½″, pieced by Barbara Gerdes Fife, machine quilted by Lee Robertson, 2016

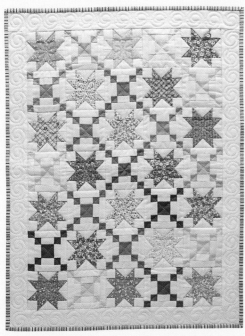

Smaller *Star Crossed*, 18½″ × 24½″, designed and pieced by Donna Lynn Thomas, partially hand-quilted by Donna Thomas, and partially machine quilted by Denise Mariano, 2017

Smallest *Star Crossed*, 10″ × 13″, machine pieced and hand quilted by Linda Birch Mooney, 2016

MATERIALS

Quilt size	Fabric A: 18 prints	Fabric B: 9 solids	Fabric C: Cream background	Backing	Binding
SMALL	8″ × 8″ square each	8″ × 8″ square each	1¼ yards	⅞ yard	¼ yard
SMALLER	7″ × 7″ square each	7″ × 7″ square each	1 yard	¾ yard	¼ yard
SMALLEST	5″ × 5″ square each	5″ × 5″ square each	½ yard	13″ × 16″	—

select fabrics

Use a different print for each of the 18 stars, 9 different solids for the 17 chain blocks, and 1 cream solid throughout. You'll have 1 leftover chain block.

CUTTING

Fabric A: From each of 18 prints	Fabric B: From each of 9 solids	Fabric C: Cream background	Backing and batting	Binding
SMALL _Finished quilt: 24½″ × 32½″_ • _Finished block: 4″ × 4″_				
Star blocks: 4 squares 2″ × 2″ ⊠ 1 square 2½″ × 2½″ for block center	**Chain blocks:** 4 strips 1¼″ × 7″ for strip sets 1 and 2 2 squares 1½″ × 1½″ for block centers	**Star blocks:** 4 strips 2″ × 40″; subcut 72 squares 2″ × 2″ ⊠ 3 strips 1½″ × 40″; subcut 72 squares 1½″ × 1½″ **Chain blocks:** 2 strips 3″ × 40″; subcut 9 strips 3″ × 7″ for strip set 1 2 strips 1½″ × 40″; subcut 9 strips 1½″ × 7″ for strip set 2 5 strips 1¼″ × 40″; subcut 36 rectangles 1¼″ × 3″ and 36 rectangles 1¼″ × 1½″ **Border:** 4 strips 2½″ × 40″	30″ × 38″ piece	4 strips 1¾″ × 40″
SMALLER _Finished quilt: 18½″ × 24½″_ • _Finished block: 3″ × 3″_				
Star blocks: 4 squares 1¾″ × 1¾″ ⊠ 1 square 2″ × 2″ for block center	**Chain blocks:** 4 strips 1″ × 5″ for strip sets 1 and 2 2 squares 1½″ × 1½″ for block centers	**Star blocks:** 4 strips 1¾″ × 40″; subcut 72 squares 1¾″ × 1¾″ ⊠ 3 strips 1¼″ × 40″; subcut 72 squares 1¼″ × 1¼″ **Chain blocks:** 2 strips 2½″ × 40″; subcut 9 strips 2½″ × 5″ for strip set 1 2 strips 1½″ × 40″; subcut 9 strips 1½″ × 5″ for strip set 2 4 strips 1″ × 40″; subcut 36 rectangles 1″ × 2½″ and 36 rectangles 1″ × 1½″ **Border:** 3 strips 2″ × 40″	23″ × 29″ piece	3 strips 1¾″ × 40″

Table continued on page 72.

Table continued from page 70.

Fabric A: From each of 18 prints	Fabric B: From each of 9 solids	Fabric C: Cream background	Backing and batting	Binding
SMALLEST *Finished quilt: 10″ × 13″* • *Finished block: 1½″ × 1½″*				
Star blocks: 4 squares 1⅜″ × 1⅜″ ◻ 1 square 1¼″ × 1¼″ for block center	**Chain blocks:** 4 strips, ¾″ × 4″ for strip sets 1 and 2 2 squares 1″ × 1″ for block centers	**Star blocks:** 3 strips 1⅜″ × 40″; subcut 72 squares 1⅜″ × 1⅜″ ◻ 2 strips ⅞″ × 40″; subcut 72 squares ⅞″ × ⅞″ **Chain blocks:** 1 strip 3″ × 40″; subcut 9 strips 1½″ × 4″ for strip set 1 and 9 strips 1″ × 4″ for strip set 2 3 strips ¾″ × 40″; subcut 36 rectangles ¾″ × 1½″ and 36 rectangles ¾″ × 1″ **Border:** 2 strips 1½″ × 40″	13″ × 16″ piece	—

Key: ◻ = Cut those squares once diagonally to make half-square triangles

make a star block

Group your pieces into 18 sets consisting of the pieces from one fabric A, and the pieces from the fabric C background print. Each set will yield 1 block. Press all the seams in the direction of the arrows indicated in the drawings. For the Smallest version, trim the seams to ⅛″ after sewing.

1 Sew the 8 fabric A and 8 fabric C background half-square triangles together on their long edges to make 8 half-square triangle units. (*Fig. A*) Press 4 to the print and 4 to the background. Trim to these sizes:

Small quilt: Trim to 1½″.

Smaller quilt: Trim to 1¼″.

Smallest quilt: Trim to ⅞″.

2 Sew the half-square triangle units into pairs as shown. *Fig. B*

3 Using the small cream squares and the larger print square, sew the rows together as shown. *Fig. C*

4 Sew the rows together to make a block. *Fig. D*

5 Repeat Steps 1–4 with each print to make a total of 18 Sawtooth Star blocks.

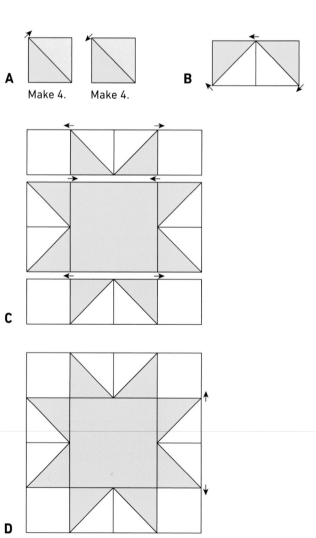

A   Make 4.   Make 4.

B

C

D

make a pair of chain blocks

Group your pieces into 9 sets consisting of the pieces from one fabric B and the pieces from the background print. Each set will yield 2 blocks. Press all the seams in the direction of the arrows indicated in the drawings. For the Smallest version, trim the seams to ⅛″ after sewing.

1 Sew 2 solid strips and the widest cream strip together to make strip set 1. (*Fig. E*) Cut 4 segments from the strip set. Refer to this list for the segment width:

Small quilt: Cut 4 segments 1¼″ wide.

Smaller quilt: Cut 4 segments 1″ wide.

Smallest quilt: Cut 4 segments ¾″ wide.

2 Sew 2 solid strips and one cream strip together to make strip set 2. (*Fig. F*) Cut 4 segments from the strip set. Refer to this list for the segment width:

Small quilt: Cut 4 segments 1¼″ wide.

Smaller quilt: Cut 4 segments 1″ wide.

Smallest quilt: Cut 4 segments ¾″ wide.

3 Sew 2 strip set 2 segments, the solid center square, and 2 short cream rectangles together into rows. *Fig. G*

4 Sew the rows together to make a nine-patch. Make 2. *Fig. H*

5 Sew 2 strip set 1 segments, 1 nine-patch from Step 4, and 2 longer cream rectangles together into rows. *Fig. I*

6 Sew the rows together to complete the block. Make 2. *Figs. J & K*

7 Repeat Steps 1–6 with each solid to make a total of 18 blocks. You will have 1 leftover block.

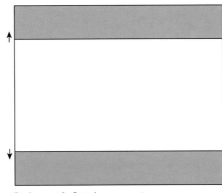

E

Strip set 1: Cut 4 segments.

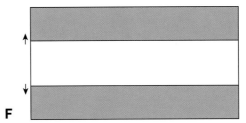

F

Strip set 2: Cut 4 segments.

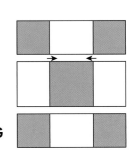

G

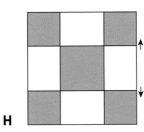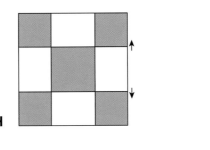

H

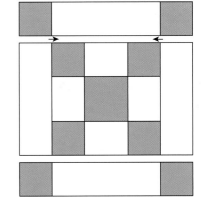

I

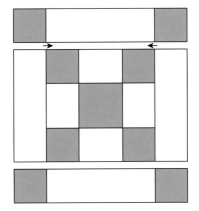

J

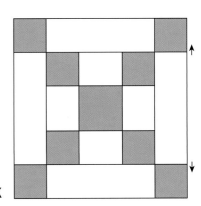

K

make the quilt top

1 Referring to the quilt diagram, arrange the Saw-tooth Star and Chain blocks alternately into 7 rows of 5 blocks. Press seams toward the Chain blocks. Sew them into rows. Join the rows together to complete the center of the quilt top.

2 Referring to Sewing Borders (page 33), measure, cut, and sew the cream border to the quilt top.

finish the quilt top

1 Layer and baste the quilt.

2 Quilt as desired.

3 Bind the quilt. Bind the Small and Smaller versions with single- or double-fold binding strips. For the Smallest version, use the backing to create a rolled binding (see Rolled Binding, page 38).

PHILADELPHIA COBBLESTONES

About 30 years ago I saw a picture of an antique Philadelphia Cobblestones quilt and have wanted to make one ever since. In these samples, Denise Mariano added a wider binding instead of a border to her Small version, and I added a skinny ¼″ pink middle border to my Smallest quilt. I really like those tiny Smallest blocks.

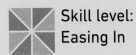 Skill level:
Easing In

Small *Philadelphia Cobblestones*, 19″ × 23⅝″, with a wider binding and omitted borders, machine pieced and quilted by Denise Mariano, 2017

Smaller *Philadelphia Cobblestones*, 20½″ × 24¼″, machine pieced and hand quilted by Linda Birch Mooney, 2016

Smallest *Philadelphia Cobblestones*, 16 x 18¾″, with an additional middle border, designed and pieced by Donna Lynn Thomas, machine quilted by Denise Mariano, 2017

MATERIALS

Quilt size	Fabric A: 10 dark prints	Fabric B: 10 light prints	Fabric C: Inner border	Fabric D: Outer border	Backing	Binding
SMALL	10″ × 10″ square	10″ × 10″ square	⅜ yard	½ yard	1 yard	¼ yard
SMALLER	10″ × 10″ square	10″ × 10″ square	9″ × 20″ piece	⅓ yard	¾ yard	¼ yard
SMALLEST	5″ × 10″ piece	5″ × 10″ piece	6″ × 20″ piece	10″ × 20″ piece	½ yard	—

select fabrics

Make 10 pairs of blocks using a different set of dark and light prints for each pair. The blocks in each pair are the mirror images of each other in terms of fabric usage. The A blocks have dark print framing strips while the B blocks are framed with the light print.

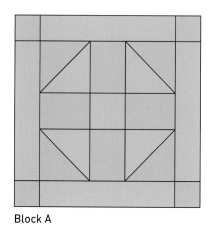
Block A

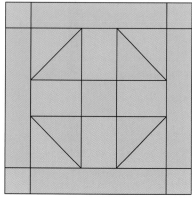
Block B

CUTTING

Fabrics A and B: From each of 10 dark prints and 10 light prints	Fabric C: Inner border	Fabric D: Outer border	Backing and batting	Binding
SMALL *Finished quilt: 27¾″ × 32⅜″ • Finished block: 4⅝″ × 4⅝″*				
4 squares 2¼″ × 2¼″ ◻ 4 rectangles 1⅜″ × 1¾″ 1 square 1⅜″ × 1⅜″ 4 rectangles 1⅛″ × 3⅞″ 4 squares 1⅛″ × 1⅛″	4 strips 2¼″ × 40″	4 strips 3⅛″ × 40″	34″ × 38″ piece	4 strips 1¾″ × 40″
SMALLER *Finished quilt: 20½″ × 24¼″ • Finished block: 3¾″ × 3¾″*				
4 squares 2″ × 2″ ◻ 4 rectangles 1¼″ × 1½″ 1 square 1¼″ × 1¼″ 4 rectangles 1″ × 3¼″ 4 squares 1″ × 1″	4 strips 1½″ × 20″	4 strips 2″ × 40″	25″ × 29″ piece	3 strips 1¾″ × 40″
SMALLEST *Finished quilt: 15½″ × 18¼″ • Finished block: 2¾″ × 2¾″*				
4 squares 1¾″ × 1¾″ ◻ 4 rectangles 1¼″ × 1″ 1 square 1″ × 1″ 4 rectangles ⅞″ × 2½″ 4 squares ⅞″ × ⅞″	4 strips 1″ × 20″	4 strips 2″ × 20″	18″ × 21″ piece	—

Key: ◻ = Cut those squares once diagonally to make half-square triangles

make a pair of blocks

Group your pieces into 10 sets consisting of the pieces from 1 fabric A and 1 fabric B. Each set will yield 2 blocks. Press all the seams in the direction of the arrows indicated in the drawings. For the Smallest version, trim the seams to ⅛" after sewing.

1 Using the fabric A and fabric B half-square triangles, make 8 half-square triangle units. *(Fig. A)* Trim to these sizes:

Small quilt: Trim to 1¾".

Smaller quilt: Trim to 1½".

Smallest quilt: Trim to 1¼".

2 Arrange the half-square triangle units, the dark and light rectangles, and center squares as shown. Sew the units into rows. *Fig. B*

3 Join the rows to complete 2 blocks. *Fig. C*

4 Repeat Steps 2 and 3 to make 2 more blocks with the fabric placement reversed. *Fig. D*

A. Make 8.

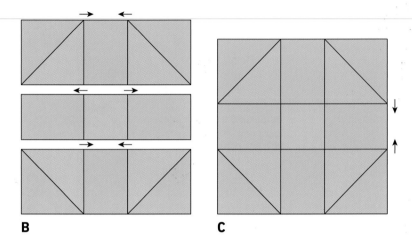

B

C

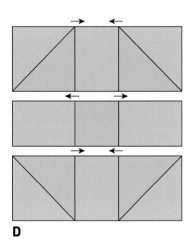

D

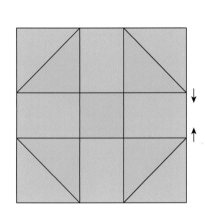

5 Sew the framing strips and squares together as shown. Sew the framing strips to the 2 blocks as shown. Press all the seams toward the long framing strips when sewing both blocks. *Fig. E*

6 Repeats Steps 5 and 6 with the fabric placement reversed. *Fig. F*

7 Repeat Steps 1–6 for each pair of blocks. Make a total of 20 blocks.

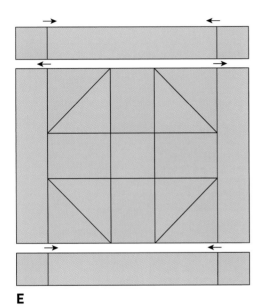
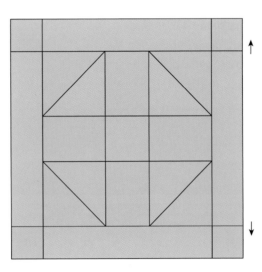

E

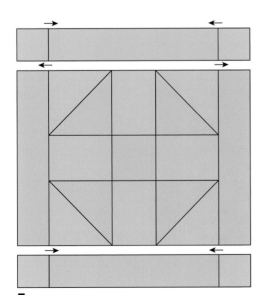
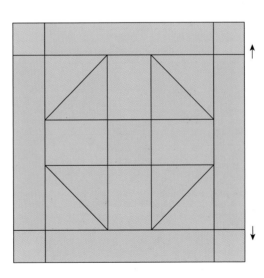

F

make the quilt top

1 Arrange the blocks into 5 rows of 4 blocks each as shown. Alternate the blocks that have dark framing strips with the ones that have light framing strips. Rotate blocks so the seams nest at the corners where the blocks meet. Balance your block colors and prints across the quilt. Sew the blocks into rows, pressing seams alternately from row to row. Join the rows together to complete the quilt top.

2 Referring to Sewing Borders (page 33), measure, cut, and sew the inner border to the quilt followed by the outer border to complete the quilt top.

finish the quilt top

1 Layer and baste the quilt.

2 Quilt as desired.

3 Bind the quilt. Bind the Small and Smaller versions with single- or double-fold binding strips. For the Smallest version, use the backing to create a rolled binding (see Rolled Binding, page 38).

'ROUND AND 'ROUND WE GO

The two samples for this project couldn't look more different, which is what makes quiltmaking infinitely fascinating. At Quilt Market in Houston one year, I bought a fat-quarter bundle of adorable, tiny woven fabrics from India. They were just the right size for my version of this quilt. Beth chose all Kaffe Fassett prints for hers, and she added a brightly colored piped binding for a touch of flair.

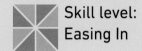 Skill level:
Easing In

Smaller *'Round and 'Round We Go*, 21⅝″ × 21⅝″, modified outer border and piped wide binding, machine pieced and machine quilted by Beth Rhodes, 2016

Smallest *'Round and 'Round We Go*, 13″ × 13″, designed and pieced by Donna Lynn Thomas, machine quilted by Theresa Ward, 2017

MATERIALS

Quilt size	Fabric A: 7 dark prints	Fabric B: Background	Fabric C: Border	Backing	Binding
SMALLER	9″ × 10″ piece each	¾ yard	⅜ yard	⅞ yard	¼ yard
SMALLEST	7″ × 7″ square each	⅜ yard	10″ × 14″ piece	16″ × 16″ square	—

select fabrics

Make the 13 blocks in 7 pairs using a different dark fabric A print for each new pair and the same fabric B background print for all the blocks. Choose a print for the fabric C border.

CUTTING

Fabric A: From each of 7 dark prints	Fabric B: Background	Fabric C: Border	Backing and batting	Binding
SMALLER *Finished quilt: 24″ × 24″ • Finished block: 4½″ × 4½″*				
8 squares 1¾″ × 1¾″ ☐ 2 strips 1″ × 10″ for strip set 2 squares 2″ × 2″	3 strips 1¾″ × 40″; subcut 56 squares 1¾″ × 1¾″ ☐ 7 strips 1″ × 40″; subcut 28 strips 1″ × 10″ for strip set 2 strips 1¼″ × 40″; subcut 28 rectangles 1¼″ × 2″ 2 squares 7⅝″ × 7⅝″ ⊠ for side setting triangles 2 squares 4⅛″ × 4⅛″ ☐ for corner triangles	3 strips 2¾″ × 40″	29″ × 29″ square	3 strips 1¾″ × 40″
SMALLEST *Finished quilt: 13″ × 13″ • Finished block: 2¼″ × 2¼″*				
8 squares 1⅜″ × 1⅜″ ☐ 2 strips ¾″ × 6″ for strip set 2 squares 1¼″ × 1¼″	2 strips 1⅜″ × 40″; subcut 56 squares 1⅜″ × 1⅜″ ☐ 5 strips ¾″ × 40″; subcut 28 strips ¾″ × 6″ for strip sets 1 strip ⅞″ × 40″; subcut 28 rectangles ⅞″ × 1¼″ 2 squares 4½″ × 4½″ ⊠ for side setting triangles 2 squares 2½″ × 2½″ ☐ for corner triangles	4 strips 2″ × 14″	16″ × 16″ square	—

Key:
☐ = Cut the squares once diagonally to make half-square triangles.
⊠ = Cut the squares twice diagonally to make quarter-square triangles.

make a pair of blocks

Group your pieces into 7 sets consisting of the pieces from 1 fabric A and the fabric B background pieces. Each set will yield 2 blocks. Press all the seams in the direction of the arrows indicated in the drawings. For the Smallest version, trim the seams to ⅛″ after sewing.

1 Using the 16 half-square triangles from 1 fabric A and 16 fabric B half-square triangles, make 16 half-square triangle units. (*Fig. A*) Trim them to these sizes:

Small quilt: Trim to 1¼″.

Smaller quilt: Trim to ⅞″.

2 Sew the half-square triangle units from Step 2 into pairs, making sure the diagonal seams nest. Make 8 pieced Flying Geese units. *Fig. B*

3 Sew a unit from Step 2 to a fabric B rectangle as shown. Make 8. *Fig. C*

4 Sew 1 fabric A strip and 2 fabric B strips together to make a strip set as shown. Make 2. (*Fig. D*) Cut 8 segments. Refer to this list for the segment width:

Smaller quilt: Cut 8 segments 2″ wide.

Smallest quilt: Cut 8 segments 1¼″ wide.

5 Arrange 1 fabric A center square, 4 strip segments, and 4 units from Step 3 as shown. Sew them into rows. *Fig. E*

6 Join the rows together to make a block. Make 2. *Fig. F*

7 Repeat Steps 1–6 to make a total of 14 blocks. You will have 1 leftover.

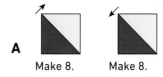

A Make 8. Make 8.

B

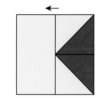

C

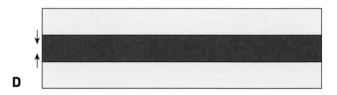

D

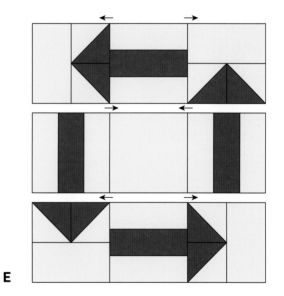

E

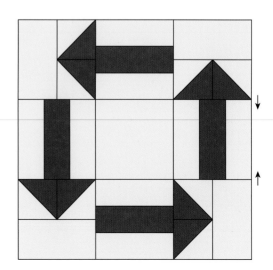

F

make the quilt top

1 Arrange the blocks and side-setting triangles into diagonal rows as shown. Rotate blocks so the seams nest at the corners where the blocks meet. Balance your block colors and prints across the quilt. Sew the blocks into rows, pressing seams alternately from row to row. Join the rows together to complete the quilt top. Add the corner triangles last.

2 Referring to Sewing Borders (page 33), measure, cut, and sew the border to the quilt.

finish the quilt top

1 Layer and baste the quilt.

2 Quilt as desired.

3 Bind the quilt. Bind the Smaller version with single- or double-fold binding strips. For the Smallest version, use the backing to create a rolled binding (see Rolled Binding, page 38).

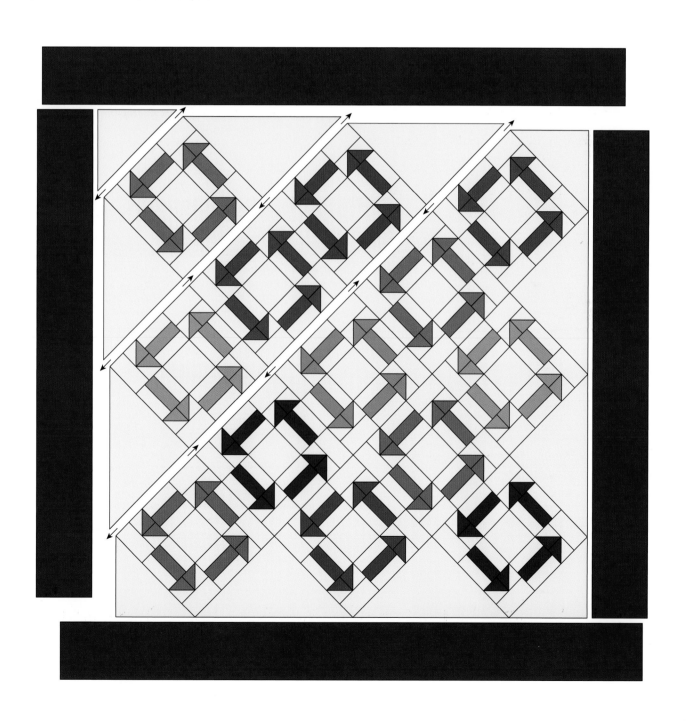

COLORED GLASS

This old block sparkles with color and lends itself to any fabric theme, whether contemporary or reproduction. How you handle the end sashing squares in this design is up to you. I kept the squares whole in the Smallest version, but the makers of the other samples chose to trim theirs off.

 Skill level:
Diving In

Small *Colored Glass*, 33½″ × 33½″, modified inner border placement, machine pieced by Beth Woods, machine quilted by Denise Mariano, 2017

Smaller *Colored Glass*, 20¾″ × 20¾″, modified inner border placement, machine pieced and hand quilted by Linda Birch Mooney, 2017

Smallest *Colored Glass*, 11½″ × 11½″, designed and pieced by Donna Lynn Thomas, machine quilted by Theresa Ward, 2017

MATERIALS

Quilt size	Fabric A: Main print 1	Fabric B: Main print 2	Fabric C: Accent print 1 and sashing squares	Fabric D: Accent print 2 and inner border	Fabric E: Background	Fabric F: Outer border and binding	Backing
SMALL	¼ yard	¼ yard	¼ yard	⅜ yard	⅞ yard	¾ yard	1¼ yards
SMALLER	9″ × 20″ piece	9″ × 20″ piece	9″ × 20″ piece	11″ × 20″ piece	½ yard	⅜ yard	¾ yard
SMALLEST	8″ × 20″ piece	8″ × 20″ piece	6″ × 20″ piece	8″ × 20″ piece	18″ × 20″ piece	9″ × 15″ piece	14″ × 14″ square

select fabrics

Choose a multicolor focus fabric for the border and, using that as a guide, choose 2 main prints, 2 accent prints, and a background print.

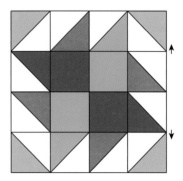

Fabric A: Main print 1 (navy in drawing)

Fabric B: Main print 2 (green in drawing)

Fabric C: Accent 1 and sashing squares (pink in drawing)

Fabric D: Accent 2 and inner border (turquoise in drawing)

Fabric E: Background print

Fabric F: Multicolor print for border and binding

CUTTING

Fabric A: Main print 1	Fabric B: Main print 2	Fabric C: Accent print 1 and sashing squares	Fabric D: Accent print 2 and inner border	Fabric E: Background	Fabric F: Outer border and binding	Backing and batting
SMALL Finished quilt: 34⅞″ × 34⅞″ • Finished block: 5″ × 5″						
1 strip 2¼″ × 40″; subcut 13 squares 2¼″ × 2¼″ ◻ 2 strips 1¾″ × 40″ for strip set	1 strip 2¼″ × 40″; subcut 13 squares 2¼″ × 2¼″ ◻ 2 strips 1¾″ × 40″ for strip set	2 strips 2¼″ × 40″; subcut 26 squares 2¼″ × 2¼″ ◻ 1 strip 1½″ × 40″; subcut 24 squares 1½″ × 1½″ for sashing squares	2 strips 2¼″ × 40″; subcut 26 squares 2¼″ × 2¼″ ◻ 4 strips 1¼″ × 40″ for inner border	5 strips 2¼″ × 40″; subcut 78 squares 2¼″ × 2¼″ ◻ 6 strips, 1½″ × 40″; subcut 36 strips 1½″ × 5½″ for sashing strips 2 squares 10″ × 10″ ⊠ for side setting triangles 2 squares 6⅛″ × 6⅛″ ◻ for corner triangles	4 strips, 3½″ × 40″ for outer border 4 strips, 1¾″ × 40″ for binding	41″ × 41″ square
SMALLER Finished quilt: 21½″ × 21½″ • Finished block: 3″ × 3″						
2 strips 1¾″ × 20″; subcut 13 squares 1¾″ × 1¾″ ◻ 2 strips 1¼″ × 20″ for strip set	2 strips 1¾″ × 20″; subcut 13 squares 1¾″ × 1¾″ ◻ 2 strips 1¼″ × 20″ for strip set	3 strips 1¾″ × 20″; subcut 26 squares 1¾″ × 1¾″ ◻ 2 strips 1″ × 20″; subcut 24 squares 1″ × 1″ for sashing squares	3 strips 1¾″ × 20″; subcut 26 squares 1¾″ × 1¾″ ◻ 4 strips 1″ × 20″ for inner border	4 strips 1¾″ × 40″; subcut 78 squares 1¾″ × 1¾″ ◻ 1 strip 3½″ × 40″; subcut 36 strips 1″ × 3½″ for sashing strips 2 squares 6⅜″ × 6⅜″ ⊠ for side setting triangles 2 squares 4″ × 4″ ◻ for corner triangles	2 strips, 2¾″ × 40″ for outer border 3 strips, 1¾″ × 40″ for binding	26″ × 26″ square
SMALLEST Finished quilt: 11½″ × 11½″ • Finished block: 1½″ × 1½″						
2 strips 1⅜″ × 20″; subcut 13 squares 1⅜″ × 1⅜″ ◻ 2 strips ⅞″ × 15″ for strip set	2 strips 1⅜″ × 20″; subcut 13 squares 1⅜″ × 1⅜″ ◻ 2 strips ⅞″ × 15″ for strip set	2 strips 1⅜″ × 20″; subcut 26 squares 1⅜″ × 1⅜″ ◻ 1 strip ¾″ × 20″; subcut 24 squares ¾″ × ¾″ for sashing squares	2 strips 1⅜″ × 20″; subcut 26 squares 1⅜″ × 1⅜″ ◻ 4 strips 1″ × 10″ for inner border	6 strips 1⅜″ × 20″; subcut 78 squares 1⅜″ × 1⅜″ ◻ 4 strips ¾″ × 20″; subcut 36 strips ¾″ × 2″ for sashing strips 2 squares 4″ × 4″ ⊠ for side setting triangles 2 squares 2½″ × 2½″ ◻ for corner triangles	4 strips, 1¾″ × 12″ for outer border No binding.	14″ × 14″ square

Key:
◻ = Cut the squares once diagonally to make half-square triangles.
⊠ = Cut the squares twice diagonally to make quarter-square triangles.

make the blocks

Press all the seams in the direction of the arrows indicated in the drawings. For the Smallest version, trim the seams to 1/8″ after sewing.

A

Fabric A: Make 26. **Fabric B:** Make 26. **Fabric C:** Make 52. **Fabric D:** Make 52.

1 Sew each of the assorted fabric A, fabric B, fabric C, and fabric D half-square triangles to a fabric E half-square triangle. (*Fig. A*) Trim to these sizes:

Small quilt: Trim to 1¾″.

Smaller quilt: Trim to 1¼″.

Smallest quilt: Trim to ⅞″.

B

2 Sew the fabric A and fabric B strips together to make 2 strips sets as shown. Press to fabric A. Cut a total of 26 segments from the strip sets. (*Fig. B*) Refer to this list for the segment width.

Small quilt: Cut 26 segments 1¾″ wide.

Smaller quilt: Cut 26 segments 1¼″ wide.

Smallest quilt: Cut 26 segments ⅞″ wide.

C

3 Sew the segments into four-patches as shown. Make 13. Pop the stitches in the center and press so the seams flow in a counterclockwise direction. *Fig. C*

D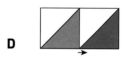

4 Sew a fabric A and fabric C half-square triangle together as shown. Make 26 pairs. *Fig. D*

5 Sew a unit from Step 4 to either side of a four-patch as shown. Make 13. *Fig. E*

E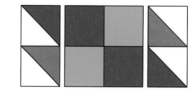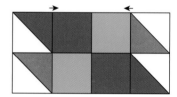

6 Arrange 2 fabric B, 2 fabric C, and 8 fabric D half-square triangle units and a unit from Step 5 as shown. Sew into rows. *Fig. F*

F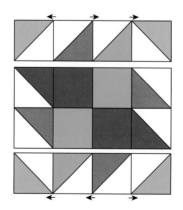

7 Join the rows together to complete a block. Make 13 blocks. *Fig. G*

G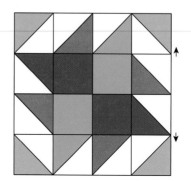

make the quilt top

1 Arrange the 13 blocks, the sashing strips, sashing squares, and side-setting triangles into diagonal rows as shown. Sew the blocks and sashing pieces into rows. *Press all the seams toward the sashing strips.* Join the rows together to complete the quilt center. Sew the 4 half-square triangles to the corners of the quilt.

2 Trim the quilt top to ¼″ from the sashing squares.

3 Referring to Sewing Borders (page 33), measure, cut, and sew the inner border into place, followed by the outer border to complete the quilt top. On the Smallest quilt, after the inner border is sewn to the quilt top, trim it to ⅝″ before sewing the outer border in place.

finish the quilt top

1 Layer and baste the quilt.

2 Quilt as desired.

3 Bind the quilt. Bind the Small and Smaller versions with single- or double-fold binding strips. For the Smallest version, use the backing to create a rolled binding (see Rolled Binding, page 38).

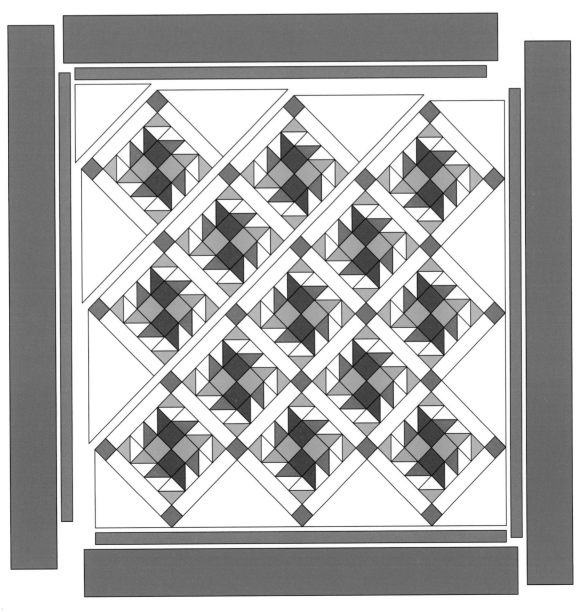

BOX OF JEWELS

Folded Box is truly my all-time favorite block. Through the careful use of value, you can create the three-dimensional effect of a box opening. By alternating it with the second block, Outward Bound, and sashings, an overall chain design appears.

For her Small sample, Doris Brown's husband, Randy, asked Doris to arrange her blocks in a specific order, rather than randomly, and she changed the center block to accommodate her design.

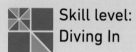 Skill level: Diving In

Small *Box of Jewels*, 34″ × 34″, with alternate blocks and modified center block, machine pieced and machine quilted by Doris Brown, 2017

Smallest *Box of Jewels*, 18¾″ × 18¾″, designed and pieced by Donna Lynn Thomas, machine quilted by Theresa Ward, 2017

Smallest *Box of Jewels*, 12¾″ × 12¾″, machine pieced and machine quilted by Doris Brown, 2017

MATERIALS

Quilt size	Fabric A: 7 dark prints for Folded Box	Fabric B: 7 medium prints for Folded Box	Fabric C: 7 light prints for Folded Box	Fabric D: 6 medium prints for Outward Bound	Fabric E: Dark print for Chains	Fabric F: Background and sashings	Fabric G: Outer border	Fabric H: Middle border	Backing	Binding
SMALL	8″ × 8″ square of each	8″ × 8″ square each	6″ × 6″ square each	10″ × 10″ square each	⅓ yard	1⅛ yards	⅜ yard	1/6 yard	1⅛ yards	¼ yard
SMALLEST	6″ × 6″ square each	6″ × 6″ square each	5″ × 5″ square each	6″ × 6″ square each	10″ × 20″ piece	⅝ yard	10″ × 20″ piece	5″ × 20″ piece	22″ × 22″ square	—

select fabrics

Make 14 Folded Box and 12 Outward Bound blocks. Use the same fabric F light background print for all 26 blocks and the sashing strips.

For the Folded Box blocks, choose a set of dark fabric A, medium fabric B, and light fabric C prints from one color family for each pair of blocks. Choose different colors for each pair. Make 7 pairs of Folded Box blocks; you will have 1 leftover block.

For the Outward Bound blocks, choose a different fabric D medium print for each pair of blocks. Use one dark fabric E print for the chains in all the Outward Bound blocks and for the sashing squares. Make 6 pairs of blocks.

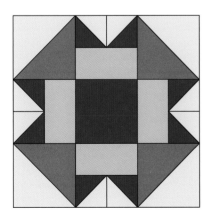

CUTTING

Fabric A: From each of 7 dark prints for Folded Box	Fabric B: From each of 7 medium prints for Folded Box	Fabric C: From each of 7 light prints for Folded Box	Fabric D: From each of 6 medium prints for Outward Bound	Fabric E: Dark print for squares in Outward Bound and sashing squares	Fabric F: Background	Fabric G: Outer border	Fabric H: Middle border	Backing and batting	Binding
SMALL Finished quilt: 34″ × 34″ • Finished block: 4½″ × 4½″									
8 squares 1¾″ × 1¾″ ◰ 2 squares 2″ × 2″ for block centers	4 squares 2½″ × 2½″ ◰	8 rectangles 1¼″ × 2″	8 rectangles 1¼″ × 2″ 8 squares 1¾″ × 1¾″ ◰	5 strips 1¼″ × 40″; subcut 7 strips 1¼″ × 20″ and 36 sashing squares 1¼″ × 1¼″ 1 strip 2″ × 40″; subcut 12 squares 2″ × 2″ for block centers	11 strips 1¼″ × 40″; subcut 7 strips 1¼″ × 20″ and 60 sashing strips 1¼″ × 5″ 6 strips 1¾″ × 40″; subcut 104 squares 1¾″ × 1¾″ ◰ 2 strips 2½″ × 40″; subcut 28 squares 2½″ × 2½″ ◰ 4 strips 1¼″ × 40″ for inner border	4 strips 2½″ × 40″	4 strips 1″ × 40″	40″ × 40″ square	4 strips 1¾″ × 40″
SMALLEST Finished quilt: 18¾″ × 18¾″ • Finished block: 2¼″ × 2¼″									
8 squares 1⅜″ × 1⅜″ ◰ 2 squares 1¼″ × 1¼″ for block centers	4 squares 1¾″ × 1¾″ ◰	8 rectangles ⅞″ × 1¼″	8 rectangles ⅞″ × 1¼″ 8 squares 1⅜″ × 1⅜″ ◰	5 strips ⅞″ × 20″ for strip sets 2 strips ⅞″ × 20″; subcut 36 sashing squares ⅞″ × ⅞″ 1 strip 1¼″ × 20″; subcut 12 squares 1¼″ × 1¼″ for block centers	7 strips ⅞″ × 40″; subcut 5 strips ⅞″ × 20″ and 60 strips ⅞″ × 2¾″ 4 strips 1⅜″ × 40″; subcut 104 squares 1⅜″ × 1⅜″ ◰ 2 strips 1¾″ × 40″; subcut 28 squares 1¾″ × 1¾″ ◰ 4 strips 1″ × 16″ for inner border	4 strips 2″ × 20″	4 strips 1″ × 20″	22″ × 22″ square	—

Key: ◰ = Cut the squares once diagonally to make half-square triangles.

make a pair of folded box blocks

Group your pieces into 7 sets consisting of the pieces from 1 fabric A, 1 fabric B, 1 fabric C, and the fabric F background pieces. Each set will yield 2 blocks. Press all the seams in the direction of the arrows indicated in the drawings. For the Smallest version, trim the seams to ⅛" after sewing.

1 Using the 2½" fabric B and fabric F half-square triangles, make 8 half-square triangle units. (Fig. A) Trim to these sizes:

Small quilt: Trim to 2".

Smallest quilt: Trim to 1¼".

2 Using the 1¾" fabric A and fabric F half-square triangles, make 16 half-square triangle units. (Fig. B) Trim to these sizes:

Small quilt: Trim to 1¼".

Smallest quilt: Trim to ⅞".

3 Sew the half-square triangles from Step 2 into pairs, arranging the pressing directions as shown. (Fig. C) Make 8 pieced Flying Geese units.

4 Sew each unit from Step 3 to a fabric C rectangle as shown. Make 8. Fig. D

5 Paying attention to pressing directions indicated by arrows in the diagram, arrange 4 large half-square triangle units, the fabric A center square, and 4 units from Step 4 as shown. Join the pieces into rows. Fig. E

6 Join the rows to complete a block. All seams should nest where they meet. Make 2. Fig. F

7 Repeat Steps 1–6 to make the remaining sets of Folded Box blocks. There will be 1 leftover block.

A
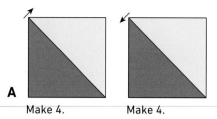
Make 4.   Make 4.

B
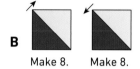
Make 8.   Make 8.

C
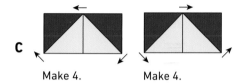
Make 4.   Make 4.

D
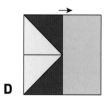

E
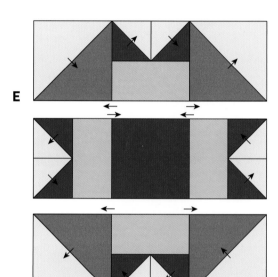

F
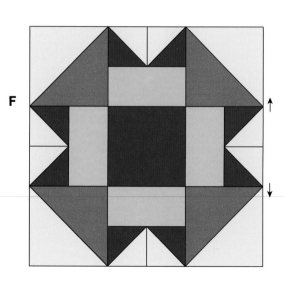

make a pair of outward bound blocks

Group your pieces into 6 sets consisting of the pieces from 1 fabric D, fabric E strips, and the fabric F background pieces. Each set will yield 2 blocks. Press all the seams in the direction of the arrows indicated in the drawings. For the Smallest version, trim the seams to ⅛″ after sewing.

G

1 Using the 20″-long fabric E and fabric F strips, make the number of strip sets indicated below. Cut a total of 96 segments from the strip sets. *Fig. G*

Small quilt: Make 7 strips sets. Cut segments 1¼″ wide.

Smallest quilt: Make 5 strip sets. Cut segments ⅞″ wide.

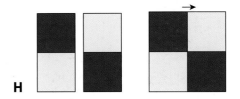

H

2 Arrange the segments as shown. Sew them into four-patches. Make 48. *Fig. H*

3 Using fabric D and fabric F half-square triangles, make 16 half-square triangle units. *(Fig. I)* Trim them to the sizes listed below.

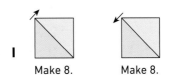

I

Make 8.   Make 8.

Small quilt: Trim to 1¼″.

Smallest quilt: Trim to ⅞″.

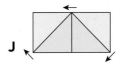

J

4 Sew the half-square triangles from Step 3 into pairs, arranging the pressing directions as shown. Make 8 pieced Flying Geese units. *Fig. J*

5 Sew a unit from Step 3 to a fabric D rectangle as shown. Make 8. *Fig. K*

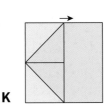

K

6 Arrange 4 four-patch units, the fabric E center square, and 4 units from Step 4 as shown. Join the pieces into rows. Orient the final four-patch seam as shown by the red lines and arrows. All seams should nest where they meet. Make 2. *Fig. L*

7 Join the rows to complete a block. *Fig. M*

8 Repeat Steps 1–6 to make the remaining sets of Outward Bound blocks.

L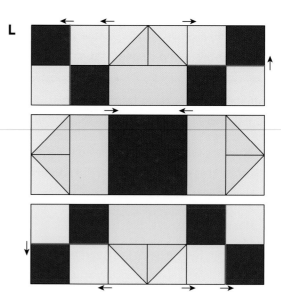

M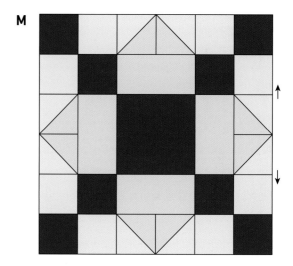

make the quilt top

1 Arrange 13 Folded Box blocks, 12 Outward Bound blocks, the sashing strips, and sashing squares into rows as shown. Sew the blocks and sashing pieces into rows. Press all the seams toward the sashing strips. Join the rows together to complete the quilt center.

2 Referring to Sewing Borders (page 33), measure, cut, and sew the inner border in place. On the Smallest quilt, after the inner border is sewn to the quilt top, trim it to ⅝″ before sewing the middle border in place.

3 Add the middle and outer borders.

finish the quilt top

1 Layer and baste the quilt.

2 Quilt as desired.

3 Bind the quilt. Bind the Small version with single- or double-fold binding strips. For the Smallest version, use the backing to create a rolled binding (see Rolled Binding, page 38).

PERKIOMEN PATHS

This split nine-patch block is fun to twist and turn into all kinds of quilt designs. Each of the project samples shows a different way to set the blocks. Try playing with your own arrangements and see what you come up with.

 Skill level:
Diving In

Small *Perkiomen Paths*, 27½″ × 27½″, machine pieced and quilted by Charlotte Freeman, 2017

Smallest *Perkiomen Paths*, 14″ × 14″, designed and machine pieced by Donna Lynn Thomas, machine quilted by Theresa Ward, 2017

Smallest *Perkiomen Paths*, 14″ × 14″, machine pieced and machine quilted by Jenise Cantlon, 2017

Small *Perkiomen Paths*, 27½″ × 27½″, machine pieced and quilted by Jenise Cantlon, 2017

MATERIALS

Quilt size	Fabric A: Main print 1	Fabric B: Main print 2	Fabric C: Accent print 1	Fabric D: Accent print 2	Fabric E: Dark print	Fabric F: Light print	Backing	Binding
SMALL	⅜ yard	⅜ yard	14″ × 20″ piece	14″ × 20″ piece	⅜ yard	⅜ yard	1 yard	¼ yard
SMALLEST	12″ × 20″ piece	12″ × 20″ piece	7″ × 20″ piece	7″ × 20″ piece	11″ × 20″ piece	11″ × 20″ piece	17″ × 17″ square	—

select fabrics

Choose 2 main color families for fabrics A and B and an accent for each of fabrics C and D. Then choose a fabric E dark print and a fabric F light print for the half-square triangle units.

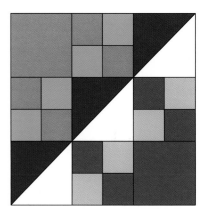

Fabric A: Main print 1 (purple in drawing)

Fabric B: Main print 2 (pink in drawing)

Fabric C: Accent 1 (orange in drawing)

Fabric D: Accent 2 (green in drawing)

Fabric E: Dark print for triangles

Fabric F: Light print for triangles

CUTTING

Fabric A: Main print 1	Fabric B: Main print 2	Fabric C: Accent print 1	Fabric D: Accent print 2	Fabric E: Dark print	Fabric F: Light print	Backing and batting	Binding
SMALL *Finished quilt: 27½″ × 27½″ • Finished block: 4½″ × 4½″*							
2 strips 2″ × 40″; subcut 36 squares 2″ × 2″ 9 strips 1¼″ × 20″ for strip set	2 strips 2″ × 40″; subcut 36 squares 2″ × 2″ 9 strips 1¼″ × 20″ for strip set	9 strips 1¼″ × 20″ for strip set	9 strips 1¼″ × 20″ for strip set	4 strips 2½″ × 40″; subcut 54 squares 2½″ × 2½″ ◻	4 strips 2½″ × 40″; subcut 54 squares 2½″ × 2½″ ◻	33″ × 33″ square	3 strips 1¾″ × 40″
SMALLEST *Finished quilt: 14″ × 14″ • Finished block: 2¼″ × 2¼″*							
3 strips 1¼″ × 20″; subcut 36 squares 1¼″ × 1¼″ 7 strips ⅞″ × 20″ for strip set	3 strips 1¼″ × 20″; subcut 36 squares 1¼″ × 1¼″ 7 strips ⅞″ × 20″ for strip set	7 strips ⅞″ × 20″ for strip set	7 strips ⅞″ × 20″ for strip set	5 strips 1¾″ × 20″; subcut 54 squares 1¾″ × 1¾″ ◻	5 strips 1¾″ × 20″; subcut 54 squares 1¾″ × 1¾″ ◻	17″ × 17″ square	—

Key: ◻ = Cut the squares once diagonally to make half-square triangles.

make the blocks

Press all the seams in the direction of the arrows indicated in the drawings. For the Smallest version, trim the seams to ⅛″ after sewing.

1 Sew the fabric A and fabric C strips into pairs to make 9 sets of strip set 1 as shown. Sew the fabric B and fabric D strips into pairs to make 9 sets of strip set 2 as shown. Press seams toward the accent prints. (*Figs. A & B*) Cut a total of 144 segments from strip sets 1 and 2. Refer to this list for the segment width:

Small quilt: Cut 144 segments 1¼″ wide.

Smallest quilt: Cut 144 segments ⅞″ wide.

2 Sew the segments into same color four-patches as shown. Make 72 of each color. Pop the seams in the center and press seams in a counterclockwise direction. *Figs. C & D*

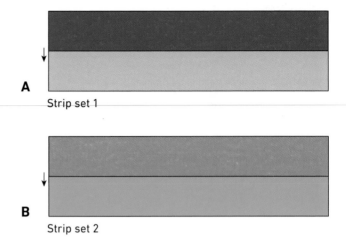

A
Strip set 1

B
Strip set 2

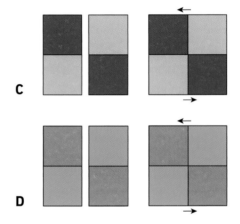

C

D

3 Sew the dark and light half-square triangles together along their long edges to make 108 half-square triangle units. Press. (*Fig. E*) Trim to these sizes:

Small quilt: Trim to 2″.

Smallest quilt: Trim to 1¼″.

E

4 Assemble the blocks as shown. Make 36. *Figs. F & G*

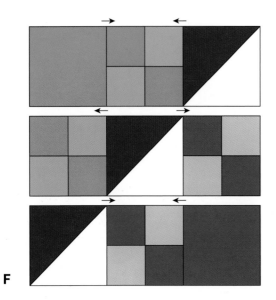

F

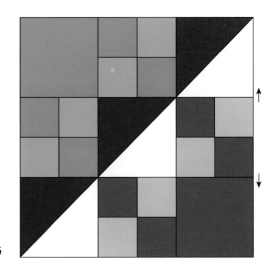

G

make the quilt top

Arrange the blocks into 6 rows of 6 blocks each, turning them as shown or into a design of your own choosing. Join the blocks into rows, pressing seams alternately from row to row. Join the rows to complete the quilt top.

finish the quilt top

1 Layer and baste the quilt.

2 Quilt as desired.

3 Bind the quilt. Bind the Small version with single- or double-fold binding strips. For the Smallest version, use the backing to create a rolled binding (see Rolled Binding, page 38).

A BIT OF THE FOURTH

Although originally designed as a patriotic mini quilt, there's no reason not to color it otherwise. If you don't wish to make the pieced border, replace it with a solid border.

 Skill level: Diving In

Small *A Bit of the Fourth*, 40″ × 40″, modified borders 3 and 5, machine pieced and machine quilted by Katharine Brigham, 2016

Smaller *A Bit of the Fourth*, 18″ × 18″, modified borders 1 and 3, omitted borders 4 and 5, machine pieced by Doris Brown, machine quilted by Denise Mariano, 2017

Smallest *A Bit of the Fourth*, 10¼″ × 10¼″, designed and pieced by Donna Lynn Thomas, machine quilted by Theresa Ward, 2017

MATERIALS

Quilt size	Fabric A: Star points	Fabric B: Star center	Fabric C: Background	Fabric D: Border and binding	Backing
SMALL	½ yard	⅜ yard	1 yard	1 yard	1⅜ yards
SMALLER	10″ × 20″ piece	10″ × 20″ piece	30″ × 20″ piece	½ yard	¾ yard
SMALLEST	9″ × 20″ piece	9″ × 20″ piece	16″ × 20″ piece	9″ × 13″ piece	13″ × 13″ square

CUTTING

Fabric A	Fabric B	Fabric C	Fabric D	Backing and batting
SMALL *Finished quilt: 39½″ × 39½″* • *Finished block: 4½″ × 4½″*				
2 strips 2½″ × 40″; subcut 26 squares 2½″ × 2½″ ◻ 2 squares 7¾″ × 7¾″ ⊠ for side setting triangles 2 squares 4¼″ × 4¼″ ◻ for corner triangles 4 squares 2½″ × 2½″ for pieced border	1 strip 2″ × 40″; subcut 13 squares 2″ × 2″ 3 strips 1½″ × 40″ for pieced border 4 strips 1″ × 40″ for border 4	2 strips 2½″ × 40″; subcut 26 squares 2½″ × 2½″ ◻ 3 strips 2″ × 40″; subcut 52 squares 2″ × 2″ 3 strips 1½″ × 40″ for pieced border 4 strips 2″ × 40″ for border 1 4 strips 1½″ × 40″ for border 3	4 strips 5½″ × 40″ for border 5 5 strips 1¾″ × 40″ for binding	45″ × 45″ square
SMALLER *Finished quilt: 20″ × 20″* • *Finished block: 2¼″ × 2¼″*				
3 strips 1¾″ × 20″; subcut 26 squares 1¾″ × 1¾″ ◻ 2 squares 4⅝″ × 4⅝″ ⊠ for side-setting triangles 2 squares 2⅝″ × 2⅝″ ◻ for corner triangles 4 squares 1½″ × 1½″ for pieced border	1 strip 1¼″ × 20″; subcut 13 squares 1¼″ × 1¼″ 4 strips 1″ × 20″ for pieced border 4 strips ¾″ × 20″ for border 4	3 strips 1¾″ × 20″; subcut 26 squares 1¾″ × 1¾″ ◻ 4 strips 1¼″ × 20″; subcut 52 squares 1¼″ × 1¼″ 4 strips 1½″ × 20″ for pieced border 4 strips 1¼″ × 12″ for border 1 4 strips 1″ × 20″ for border 3	4 strips 3″ × 20″ for border 5 3 strips 1¾″ × 40″ for binding	25″ × 25″ square
SMALLEST *Finished quilt: 10¼″ × 10¼″* • *Finished block: 1⅛″ × 1⅛″*				
2 strips 1⅜″ × 20″; subcut 26 squares 1⅜″ × 1⅜″ ◻ 2 squares 2⅞″ × 2⅞″ ⊠ for side setting triangles 2 squares 1¾″ × 1¾″ ◻ for corner triangles 4 squares 1″ × 1″ for pieced border	1 strip ⅞″ × 20″; subcut 13 squares ⅞″ × ⅞″ 4 strips ¾″ × 12″ for pieced border 4 strips 1″ × 10″ for border 4	2 strips 1⅜″ × 20″; subcut 26 squares 1⅜″ × 1⅜″ ◻ 3 strips ⅞″ × 20″; subcut 52 squares ⅞″ × ⅞″ 4 strips ¾″ × 12″ for pieced border 4 strips 1¼″ × 7″ for border 1 4 strips 1¼″ × 10″ for border 3	4 strips 1¾″ × 12″ for border 5 No binding	13″ × 13″ square

Key:
◻ = Cut the squares once diagonally to make half-square triangles.
⊠ = Cut the squares twice diagonally to make quarter-square triangles.

make the block

Press all the seams in the direction of the arrows indicated in the drawings. For the Smaller and Smallest versions, trim the seams to ⅛″ after sewing.

A

1 Sew the fabric A triangles and the fabric C triangles together on their long edges to make 52 half-square triangle units. (*Fig. A*) Trim to these sizes:

Small quilt: Trim to 2″.

Smaller quilt: Trim to 1¼″.

Smallest quilt: Trim to ⅞″.

2 Using the fabric B squares, fabric C squares, and the half-square triangle units from Step 1, assemble 13 Star blocks as shown. *Figs. B & C*

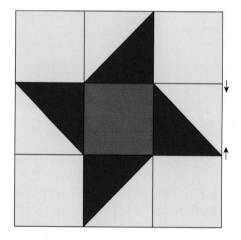

B

make the quilt top

1 Sew the fabric A side setting triangles and 13 blocks together in diagonal rows as shown. Join the rows to complete the center of the quilt. Add the corner triangles last. Trim the quilt center to ¼″ from the block corners before sewing on the borders. *Fig. D*

2 Sew the fabric C border 1 strips to the quilt center (see Sewing Borders, page 33).

For the Smallest quilt, border 1 is cut oversized. The quilt center should measure 4¾″ finished size (5¼″ with seams) at this point. Once the border is sewn in place, trim it to measure ⅝″ from the seam if your quilt center was the correct size. If not, trim the Smallest quilt to 6″ square (3″ from center to raw edges on all sides) so the pieced border will fit next to it.

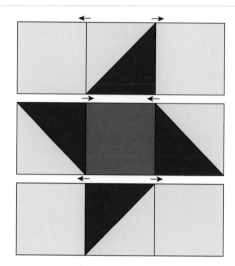

C

D

3 Sew the fabric B and fabric C strips for the pieced border into pairs to make 3 strip sets for the Small quilt and 4 for the Smaller and Smallest quilts. (*Fig. E*) Cut a total of 44 segments for all quilt sizes. Refer to this list for the segment width:

E

Small quilt: Cut 44 segments 2½″ wide.

Smaller quilt: Cut 44 segments 1½″ wide.

Smallest quilt: Cut 44 segments 1″ wide.

F

4 Sew 11 segments together to make a pieced border. Make 4 borders. *Fig. F*

5 Referring to Sewing Borders (page 33), sew the pieced borders, corner squares, and remaining borders 3–5 to the quilt top to complete it.

Border 3 on the Smallest quilt is cut oversized. Sew it in place, press, and trim to measure ½″ from the seam. Then continue adding borders 4 and 5.

Border 4 on the Smallest quilt is cut oversized. Sew it in place, press, and trim to measure ⅜″ from the seam. Then continue adding border 5. *Fig. G*

finish the quilt top

1 Layer and baste the quilt top.

2 Quilt as desired.

3 Bind the quilt. Bind the Small and Smaller versions with single- or double-fold binding strips. For the Smallest version, use the backing to create a rolled binding (see Rolled Binding, page 38).

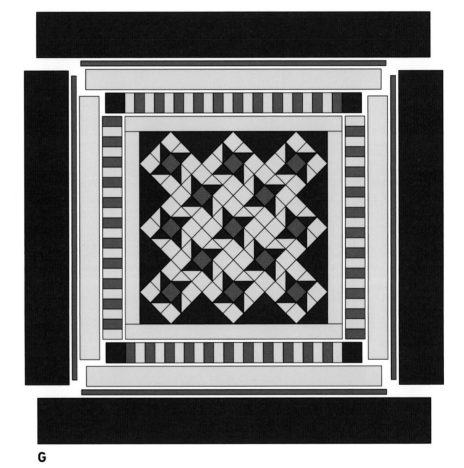

G

ABOUT THE AUTHOR

DONNA LYNN THOMAS has been sewing since the age of four and passionately quilting since 1975. She began teaching in 1982, and as an army wife, lived in Germany for four years where she thoroughly enjoyed teaching at a German quilt shop and various guilds throughout the country. Now out of the army, the Thomases have settled in Kansas. Donna continues to teach and speak nationally.

Donna places a strong focus on mastering basic and precision skills, not to please the quilt police, but rather to help quilters reduce frustration and better enjoy the creative process.

The author of 18 quilt books since the late 1980s, Donna continues to write and contribute articles to various quilt-related publications. Currently she writes the column Quilting Fundamentals for *Modern Quilts Unlimited*. Donna also teaches an online class, Piece Like a Pro, that you can watch on Craftsy.

Her greatest joy is her husband, Terry, and their two sons, Joe and Pete. Equally dear to her heart are her daughters-in-law, both named Katie, and Donna's most-perfect-in-every-way granddaughters, Charlotte and Alexandra.

Donna and Terry provide staff assistance to their two cats, Max and Skittles, and a kiddie pool and ear scratches to one sunny golden retriever, Ellie. All the quilts in their house are lovingly "pre-furred."

Visit Donna online!

Website: donnalynnthomasquilter.com

Facebook: /donnalynnthomasquilter

Instagram: @dtdonna55

Photo by Lifetouch

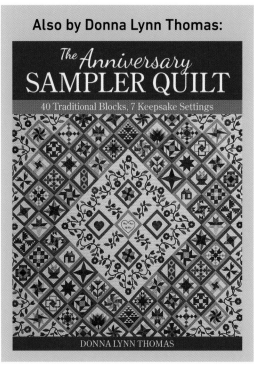

Also by Donna Lynn Thomas:

The Anniversary SAMPLER QUILT

40 Traditional Blocks, 7 Keepsake Settings

DONNA LYNN THOMAS

Want even more creative content?

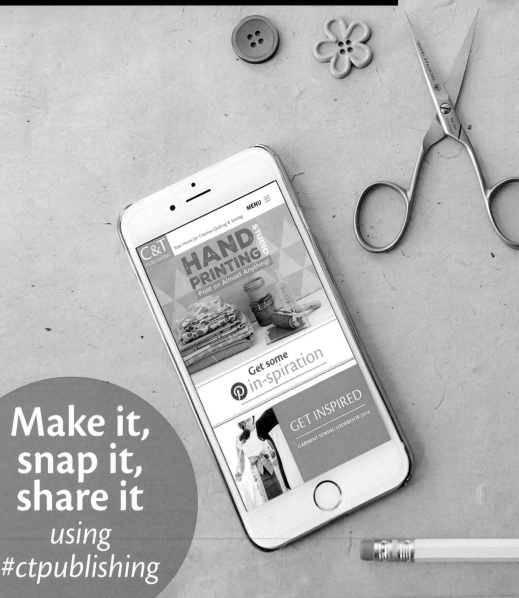

Make it, snap it, share it
*using
#ctpublishing*